COOKING IN THE COUNTRY

Cooking in the Country

TOM JAINE

With an introduction by CHRISTOPHER DRIVER
Photographs by JAMES RAVILIOUS

Chatto & Windus LONDON

Published in 1986 by Chatto & Windus Ltd
40 William IV Street, London WC2N 4DF

British Library Cataloguing in Publication Data
Jaine, Tom
    Cooking in the country.
    1. Cookery, British   2. Restaurants,
    lunch rooms, etc.——Great Britain
    I. Title
    641.5′0941   TX717

ISBN 0–7011–3134–9

Printed in Great Britain by
Redwood Burn Limited, Trowbridge, Wiltshire

FILIABUS DILECTISSIMIS

CONTENTS

PUBLISHER'S NOTE
AND OVEN TEMPERATURE CHART

Imperial and metric measurements are given in these recipes. The metric equivalents vary somewhat; for instance, in some recipes 30g is given as an approximate equivalent for 1oz, while in others 25g is preferred. This is a matter of taste. Use one or other set of measurements; do not mix the two.

It should be remembered that the American pint is 16fl oz in comparison to the Imperial pint, used in both Britain and Australia, which is 20fl oz. The British standard tablespoon which has been used in this book holds 17.7ml, the American 14.2ml, and the Australian 20ml. A teaspoon holds approximately 5ml in all three countries.

Oven temperature chart

°C	°F	Gas mark	
110	225	$\frac{1}{4}$	very slow
130	250	$\frac{1}{2}$	
140	275	1	slow
150	300	2	
170	325	3	
180	350	4	moderate
190	375	5	
200	400	6	moderately hot
220	425	7	hot
230	450	8	
240	475	9	very hot

ACKNOWLEDGEMENTS

I am grateful to the following whose work is here quoted or between whose covers some of my pages have first appeared: Dartington Rural Archive, Ted Hughes, Gay Lange, Alan Davidson and *Petits Propos Culinaires*, the International Wine & Food Society and their *World Gastronomy 1986*. The following cookery writers have been shamelessly plagiarised: Elizabeth Ayrton, Elizabeth David, Jane Grigson and Constance Spry. Many others have been plundered; I hope proper acknowledgement is made in the relevant recipes.

This book would not exist without the work of three people, my former partners Joyce Molyneux, Heather Crosbie and George Perry-Smith. Their example has been my tutor and it is to illuminate some tithe of it that I turned to words. Nor would I have continued without the support of the subscribers to *Twelve Times a Year* and of its occasional, and much valued, contributors. Other writers, more skilled than me, have been of great help: Lynda Brown, Alan and Jane Davidson, Christopher Driver. They are not responsible for any faults. I am grateful to Clare Pawley for help with research, and to Hilary Laurie at Chatto & Windus for her sensitive and cheerful patience.

All would be nought were it not for my wife, Sally.

ALLALEIGH HOUSE 1985–86

Here are a few silly propositions which, if you were brought up in Britain, you may have been conned into believing:

It must be good if so much of it is sold.

No one bright enough to have the choice goes into catering.

Restaurants are not worth reading about unless you can afford to eat in them twice a week.

People who do, can't teach. People who teach, can't do.

Let's wait until the production gets to London.

Once a generation or so some person or close-knit group arises to knock all these propositions down in prose as craftsmanlike as their practice. For food and innkeeping, crusty John Fothergill achieved it half a century ago with his best-selling *Innkeeper's Diary*. A quarter-century ago, George Perry-Smith of the Hole in the Wall in Bath had all the qualifications except the writerly conviction that someone would listen to him. Now, Perry-Smith's stepson and former partner Tom Jaine has set down how he and his colleagues in their turn built up in Dartmouth a restaurant as stylish, rooted and individual as Chez Panisse in California or the Hotel de la Gare in Digoin or Berowra Waters outside Sydney.

Well before I knew Tom Jaine as a writer and antiquary, or indeed his kitchen partner Joyce Molyneux as a creative cook in her own right, I used to write annual *Good Food Guide* entries about their Carved Angel. These descriptions expressed not my own (alas) occasional experience but better judges' or more regular visitors' affection for a restaurant whose cooking matched in its own style the quality that the big-name London French had begun to achieve with their huge advantages of investment, trained brigades and ready access to prime materials. But I had no illusion that the production could ever be translated to London or the home counties, even if the impresarios had wanted to shake off the sticky soil and tangled fishing nets of Devon. A restaurant of this stature depends not just on recipes and stove technique but on an intricate network of producer–consumer relationships. It is these that make Tom's mannered but precise pages so delightful and informative for anyone who notices what they eat and cook, and so instructive to any young man or woman in or out of the catering trade whose fondest dream is a restaurant of their own one day.

Some will turn first in this book to the recipes adopted or evolved at the Carved Angel; others to the owner's abrasive comments on the performance of his kitchen machinery; others again to his lively small talk – so reminiscent of that Devon classic, *Small Talk at Wreyland* – about spinach or salmon or kid's offal; the kind of market and tasting notes which seldom surface in cookery books, let alone in college texts for the under-educated young people who most need leading down these byways. But for me perhaps the chief pleasure of Tom's book is the eye he keeps on the truth that cooking, however grandly achieved, finally has to be set before a live customer who sits at table with an appetite and a purse, hoping to have the one satisfied and the other spared unnecessary depletion. I have waited for years to hear this from a professional caterer in this country, be his origin British, French or Italian.

'One result of an unhealthy emphasis on the art rather than the fact of food has been to make restaurant meals less digestible than domestic ones. There is a constant pressure to elaborate or enrich, no matter whether the chef subscribes to the tenets of *nouvelle cuisine*. Four out of five meals in restaurants leave me half dead for twelve hours. I have never understood why. It is neither food poisoning nor excessive alcohol. My appetite, at home, is gargantuan. Yet, if the same approach is followed at restaurants, nemesis will follow.'

Even Tom cannot find a cure for these symptoms, any more than he can fully explain why British restaurants and hotels are so horrible to families with young children. (On my first – anonymous – visit to the Carved Angel, the ten-year-old we had with us broke a wine glass. Their reaction to this mishap made her their friend for life.) But if common-sense, curiosity and a trained mind can do something to raise the sights and enlarge the horizons of a trade which sells us so much food and drink so successfully and so mechanically, Tom Jaine will have put us all in his debt.

Christopher Driver
(Editor of *Guardian* Food and Drink.
Author of *The British at Table 1940–1980*)

January

In 1980, the depths of the year, I was casting around for things to do. Winter in Dartmouth has this effect. The town hibernates. Shops close for an extra half day; customers are sparse. You can walk up the main street at five in the afternoon and see no one. The restaurant too is quiet, if not set to idle. The summer staff have fled to bright lights and prosperity. For those who remain the prospect of holidays, in January, is there. My partner, Joyce Molyneux, keeps hands active, turned to winter tasks such as two hundred Christmas puddings for David Mellor, the cutlery and kitchen shop in London and Manchester. Long nights set one dreaming: of fame and fortune, of more customers next summer, of ways and means to bring them in. Thus was *Twelve Times a Year* started, as a publicity sheet or newsletter by subscription.

Broad content has been unchanging while the emphasis shifts according to enthusiasms; always a report on shopping and the state of supplies; always a few recipes; always an article or two about a particular supplier or commodity; almost always something about wine; the bulk written by me. This book is a collection from this newsletter. The monthly diaries are amalgams and selections from the shopping reports of five years. Some attempt has been made, in their selection, to reflect the constant cycle of the seasons and the variations of the weather from year to year. This has an effect both on the condition of the raw materials, on our own spirits and the health of our business.

I make reference to two restaurants: the Carved Angel and the Tall Ships, sitting at each end of the river front at Dartmouth. Although the first was the true centre of our activity, the second had its importance. I opened it as a cheaper restaurant, offering almost exclusively fish, in 1982. It played its part by demonstrating the problems of large numbers of customers and cooking cheaper sorts of fish in a palatable form. Equally, it showed the difficulty of doing two things at once.

People sometimes object that recipes written for or by restaurants are unusable in the home or, at best, feasible only for the grandest and

Joyce Molyneux of the Carved Angel.

most time-consuming occasions. They have some justification. The restaurant kitchen is able to spread its resources across a wide band of dishes, so sharing the cost of luxuries between several tables and dishes. The domestic manager, faced with a recipe calling for a teaspoonful of caviar, is forced to buy an ounce at extortionate cost or ignore the instruction. Either way is less than satisfactory. In equal measure, the restaurant cook can make a single task serve several ends. The day's preparation may consist of twenty items which, by varying combinations, may produce thirty dishes. As the number of mouths at home never matches that of a busy restaurant, each cooking process will have but one end in view. This makes some recipes unnecessarily labour intensive.

But a word of defence before the gentle reader discards all these instructions! The main difference between the professional and the domestic cook is that of attitude and routine, not methods or materials. To make sense of the day's activity, it must be planned and considered. A job done at nine in the morning may not have its pay-off until late in the night. Waste or surplus from one process may be turned to some use in another. This economy of effort is not laziness but forethought. All too often, when turning in one's own kitchen to prepare the next meal, no longer perspective intrudes on the task in hand. So a stock is made, but only partly used; a packet is opened, for but a scraping of ingredient; the store cupboard is shown once again to be bare of the essential spice or flavouring; everything has to be done from scratch. The meal, then, takes two hours to prepare and but fifteen minutes to eat. Why bother? Well, there is the question of enjoyment; then the consideration that it may be easier than this if meals are treated as groups, not as unique entities.

The recipes here may have been used in a restaurant, but are in the tradition of Elizabeth David and Jane Grigson, both authors writing for a domestic audience. One of the changes that came about in British eating after the last war was the de-professionalising of personnel, materials and methods. So there is no reason why a book should not serve both markets. A contrary tendency can now be described, as the influence of the great French restaurants becomes more accessible through press and television. This shift in fashion has extended to shops and to the private household.

THE CARVED ANGEL RESTAURANT

The Carved Angel is a small restaurant fronting the river at Dartmouth (pop. 6298) in South Devon. It serves food of all sorts, drawing from the recipes of Europe for its menus, much in the manner of late twentieth century English cookery. If it seems French in style, though nothing could be less French, this is due to the influence exerted by that nation over matters culinary, as well as our own propensities. But it is peculiarly English, not British, beneath that veneer of the foreign wished upon it by the restaurant culture of which it is part as well as by the customers who want it thus.

It began in July 1974. Actual possession was taken in December 1973, not long before the imposition of the three-day week by Edward Heath. A winter of strange events, overheard on the radio as we squelched at the bottom of a three-foot trench attempting to make a junction with the main drain beneath a tidal pavement.

The partners were four in number: Heather Crosbie, Joyce Molyneux, George Perry-Smith and Tom Jaine. The source and origin of the venture was the Hole in the Wall in Bath. This, a long-standing restaurant in the centre of the city (wistfully remembered by members of the armed forces for years after Hitler's war) was taken over by George Perry-Smith in the early fifties. The trajectory of its career has often been described. Although an amateur in the strict sense, none could have been more professional. George Perry-Smith brought a Gallic sense of exuberance and enthusiasm for food and its service to a community long nurtured on stuffed shirts and tired grills. This was applied single-mindedly to the creation of a restaurant and to working in a restaurant, without dissipation of the concentration into marketing or management, the usual professional failing. The result was astonishingly successful, the more so as the hedonist sixties supplanted the post-war years. In the last years of that decade, Heather Crosbie and Joyce Molyneux were brought into the partnership. The Bath restaurant was sold in 1972, the partnership dissolved.

It was always a probability that another place would be started, although the inclination of the original partners was to draw back from a new venture. Life at the Hole in the Wall had consumed opportunities of self-expression save through the restaurant itself. Too successful and too dependent on personal involvement to admit of any respite, like a juggernaut, it trundled forward. However, tax liabilities meant something had to be undertaken within an allotted span. It was thought, perhaps, that if a smaller place were found, less subjugation to its demands might be the outcome. In the long run this principle proved fallacious; it is all proportionate. Heather Crosbie favoured a south-western location, ideally rural. They found the Riverside, in Helford village in Cornwall. No spot could be more idyllic, a greater summation of the Englishman's cottage in a country setting. Riverside was a going concern, in the capable hands of the Munros. It needed, therefore, little work before restarting in a new guise. Since then, the work of the partners has been to create a set of bedrooms to entice people to the western edge of England while continuing to cook as they know best. It is undeniably popular; the warmth of the welcome reinforced by dinner table and breakfast tray, bathed in the light and peace of the Lizard: a potent cocktail.

That the same partnership should have a restaurant at Dartmouth came from a conjunction of events. Tom Jaine, step-son of George Perry-Smith and an archivist by trade, had taken advantage of the great property boom in London to bolster his lowly status in the civil service against the onslaught on inflation. However, capital appreciation was soon spent and the cycle of reinvestment and return slowed down. The prospect of shifting from salaried to self-employed was irresistible. It was mooted that if the partnership expanded from two or three to four, there would be opportunity to operate two restaurants, to the benefit of all. The search that had ended at Helford had also taken in Dartmouth where there was a small restaurant called Glenies coming up for auction. A revisit was proposed and a successful bid entered. The rules of engagement were that Helford would be the domain of George Perry-Smith and Heather Crosbie and Dartmouth of Joyce Molyneux and Tom Jaine. The profits would be shared. The waiting time, while Dartmouth was reconstructed, would be spent by Joyce at Helford. Opening was scheduled for Easter 1974. In the event, building took some months more.

Although Glenies had been successful in its heyday, it had fallen on bad times. There was little mileage to be obtained from its goodwill. A complete change was envisaged: the name, the structure, the style. Unless physical alteration is radical, the hangover from previous occupants can be oppressive. There is a degree to which the Carved Angel was intended as a statement, certainly clear in my mind if not in other people's. But first, the name and motif: there is absolutely no significance in the name the Carved Angel. The restaurant was called Glenies after its former proprietors. Many places in the sixties used this form, as indeed had the world since the dawn of time. However, the practice seemed especially redolent of that bubble of bistros and small personality restaurants that opened in that decade. The building we occupied had no history; it was a modern construction, in the Tudor style, dating only from the embanking of the river front at the end of the last century. There was no inspiration to be drawn from that. In the event, a trawl of signs or signboards was made in a list of eighteenth-century furniture makers compiled by Ambrose Heal. The Carved Angel was selected on the one hand for its charm and on the other because a friend of the partnership, the late Bill Haines, was willing and able to execute the carving that now stands in the dining room. The intention was to attach it to the outside of the building. However, reasons of weather and security intruded.

The design of the restaurant was central to any intended statement. It should be modern, in the brave Habitat manner, though nothing came from Habitat itself. It should eschew the gentility of the classic restaurants and grand hotels. It should have a slightly metropolitan air, even though in the country, while preserving something of the domestic scale in keeping with its size. The mixture, in the long term, is still quintessentially English though avoiding the excesses of post-modern architecture (then barely thought about) and the beloved chintzy look of Laura Ashley. When we first opened, the room was bare, if not gaunt. There were no table cloths, there was little in the way of picture and ornament, there was no break between the restaurant and kitchen, even below waist height. As the years passed, the room filled up and mellowed, took on that tone of pine, brass and linen that it has now. The most fervent of programmists are changed little by little.

Nonetheless, the nature of the dining room was indelibly affected by the vistas at each end. To the outside, there was a great picture window, the former shop window, opening on to a river and its traffic. This was hidden by curtains come the night, but there was no other impediment to the sensation of living in an aquarium. The internal vista was the kitchen, totally open to diners' inspection. Indeed, it intruded upon it. This too was by design, a holistic approach to cooking and eating, intended for the benefit of the customer, staff and owners. The ideal was that the food should be cooked with art but no artifice; that the customer's order should have a direct and perceptible effect on the kitchen; that the customer should in turn receive his food with no unnecessary ceremony; that some of the cobwebs of obfuscation and barriers to communication should thus be lowered.

There were greater ambitions. These revolved round the modern preoccupation with reproducing a French arcadia in an English town, the ideal of the French café-restaurant embedded in the life of the community, open to all comers, ever willing to please and produce. The vibrancy of the community itself will spill over into the restaurant; the two will be locked in a symbiotic spiral towards excellence. This view, I think, comes from the exposure of British youth to French culture. At the age of twenty, the café is seductive; drinking all hours, pavement life. Further, the cafés that one frequented were haunted by like minds. The image engendered the fact. The philosophic banter came not from the café, but its occupants. The same process may explain the attraction of the English public house to university students. As adulthood creeps in, the French café loses much of its charm; its nature more nearly approaches that of any other drinking house, filled by people of a somewhat *louche* nature, seeking solace on the zinc. Furthermore, the French restaurant, if serious in intent, is as socially divisive or restrictive as any English one – even if certain manifestations, for instance rules about clothing, are rarely seen. Closer inspection also shows that French customers are categorised, even vilified, by the restaurateur much as in England and that they behave in the same demanding, hectoring and demoralising way as customers the world over. In France, as in Britain, the customer is what you deserve; if you welcome him and love him, he welcomes and loves you. An indomitable optimism about human nature is a compulsory attribute in catering. Pessimism, engendering as it does less lovable responses in your clientele, is rewarded by nervous collapse.

The ambition subsisted while alterations were in progress. Here was a small town that could take to its heart a small restaurant. If we opened our doors at all hours; if we offered a menu of broad enough spectrum; if we designed a café as well as a restaurant area, we could be part of that community. It proved impossible of execution. Not only was the space not there, but it became plain that it is not feasible to mix modes of expression. The history of the restaurant is, in one way, that of increasing exclusivity. For the first two years of our time, we served morning coffee, a gesture towards our arcadia. The number of people who took advantage of this was small; however, our presumptions on that score would be overturned of a Sunday morning when coachloads of people might suddenly appear demanding a restorative cup. All life must stop while they are satisfied. Sunday lunch, always a busy meal, could not be prepared until they left. This would leave a quarter of an hour to hoover, clean and lay up. If we took £5, we were lucky. We stopped the gesture. Exclusion began with things like that; it continued with gradually restricted opening hours – never to the extent of dinner at 8.00, but certainly closing for lunch at 1.45. The pricing policy also had this effect. When we opened, it cost about £5 per head for a dinner. By 1985 this had risen to £25, still cheap in national terms, but made difficult to duck by having a single price for the whole meal rather than *à la carte* divisions. As the restaurant became more popular, so it became unlikely that a chance passer-by would obtain a seat. Hardly our fault, but a regrettable development.

The origins of the cooking style practised by Joyce Molyneux need little rehearsal. Elizabeth David's portraits of a Mediterranean world of robust flavour and colour; her description of French provincial cookery; the English appreciation of things foreign and things with a country rather than metropolitan sophistication; the reappraisal of English food that has been led by Elizabeth David and Jane Grigson – all have contributed their knowledge and enthusiasm to a classical English training and to a career radically affected by the perceived success of these traits at the Hole in the Wall. It is interesting to watch how Joyce Molyneux's cooking has developed away from the initial source, George Perry-Smith's, since her establishment at Dartmouth in 1974. There has been a greater receptivity to *nouvelle cuisine*, even if it shows in less than fashionable ways. The great series of French chefs' recipe books, starting with Guérard and continuing with Troisgros, Vergé and so on, has had its effect. Similarly, the interest of British writers in spices and sweeter flavours to savoury dishes has been reflected more at Dartmouth than at Helford. However, the common source is still perceived. Customers with no idea of a connection will suggest that Dartmouth has overtones of Helford and *vice versa*. It comes from attitudes: to the customer, to the business of serving food and that of buying it. It also comes from being embedded in a time-warp. Both restaurants were started before the transformation of the English scene by the new French stars in London and the provinces and the creation of the country house hotel. These are the *leitmotifs* of the late seventies. Dartmouth and Helford are creatures of the sixties, before new methods of finance and new horizons of wealth from tourism created new forms of expression. That they are still valid, still successful and still enjoyable is a measure of the potency of the image first worked out in the years after the second world war.

My own connection with the partnership has ceased. A solipsist's life in the country offered a temporary alternative. This book is a record of that connection – not regretted, much missed, while recognising that food and its service is not the be-all and end-all of human existence.

BUYING MATERIALS

There is an analogy between the chef and the painter and decorator. If the latter fails to make good, the finish he can achieve on the last coat will be compromised. So too the chef; he may be a genius at the stove, but no amount of seasoning will lift second-rate materials bought unthinkingly from an uncaring wholesaler. The misquoted adage, 'first catch your hare', says it all. The first, and maybe most essential, part of a successful recipe is procurement. Of course, if the materials are of high enough standard, the degree of change implicit in cooking and flavouring may be lessened so that the taste of the original may shine through. Much of the new cooking depends on a revitalised appreciation of the quality and range of materials, especially in England. Outlandish combinations may come from a new confidence in the ability of greengrocers and fruiterers to deliver exotics in better condition than ever before. Equally, if some of the more modish recipes are attempted with frozen shellfish or dried herbs the result is more disastrous than it ever used to be when Pellaprat and the *Répertoire* were the sole occupants of the kitchen library. *La cuisine du marché* is an accurate term; chefs are attempting to find fresh food to be cooked the same day, no substitutes allowed.

It would be unjust, however, to claim that it is our generation of cooks that has discovered the need for good materials, though what has happened of late may be distinguished from earlier cycles of renewal and improvement. Firstly, we have overcome the reaction to the dearth and despair of the war and the post-war. Not only did food quality decline, imports cease, substitutes gain acceptance, but luxury became somehow dishonest. Quality, regrettably, became synonymous with luxury. So the man who would not brook frozen lamb was not making a stand for things right and proper, rather he was undermining the fabric of society. This is a generational attitude; it is now passing. Secondly, the last twenty years have seen a great increase in the range of materials available to us. Imports are trunked by road and air, arriving in better condition than ever used to be the case; cuisines of other cultures have gained acceptance, giving rise to the adoption of a number of ingredients, edible plants and styles; new varieties of fruits have been developed and grown commercially. A third aspect is our current preoccupation with bodily health and its links with diet. As raw foods gain in popularity, so does the demand for good quality. The consumer desires, even needs, to know the origin and nature of the ingredients of his meal.

Tom Laughton wrote in *Pavilions By The Sea* (1977) of his introduction to hotel-keeping in Edwardian Scarborough in the hands of his father. The excellence of the food was mainly due to his expert marketing, which obtained for the kitchens all the best local produce. Every morning he set off from the hotel at six-thirty as the shop shutters were being taken down, to make sure that he had first choice from what the tradesmen had to offer. The early morning expedition is a constant of most chefs' lives, though in Laughton's case it was the proprietor who did the buying. In large cities, the round may be restricted to the markets, but the number of places where this may be achieved is shrinking with the changing pattern of trade. Nowadays, too many of the provincial markets are mere outposts, and inferior ones at that, of the London nexus. You are better off buying direct from Covent Garden. London (in restaurant terms) has almost become an outpost of Rungis market in Paris – which in turn dominates the provincial network of France. But, in a small town in the English countryside, a morning constitutional is useless for there are few shops and less choice. The routine of shopping and procurement is quite different.

This principle was recognised by the pre-war country restaurateur *par excellence*, John Fothergill. 'When I took this shop, I thought round for all the things I had found best wherever I'd been and sent for them. So Kate pays regular bills for food stuff in Athens, France, Norway, Jaffa and Italy. And of English things we have daily from three bakers three different kinds of bread made from flours that I have forced upon them, besides the breads we make ourselves, cheese from East Harptree, salt from Maldon, mustard from Newport Pagnell, sausages, after a romantic search all over England, from Glenthorn in Thame, books from the Book Society, bacon found by accident, from the International Stores, . . . and despite the trouble, the net result upon the patient is that he is alive to something very different in the food.'

Much the same process might be said to have occurred when we began buying for the Carved Angel, save that the background of the partnership as a whole offered more experience of food and foodstuffs than Fothergill had when he started at the Spreadeagle, Thame, in the

1920s. But the resources immediately available left much to be desired: butchers who took meat as delivered to them by the wholesaler; greengrocers that had no thought to size or quality, only price; catering suppliers of larder goods dealing in the most impoverished of brands. In part, the fault was down to them but almost as much blame attaches to their customers. Pre-occupation with price resulted, for example, in most English kitchens accepting catering block chocolate. The effect on a serious chocolate dessert is cataclysmic. The same process is observable with wine – provided it is called Niersteiner, the cheapest is acceptable, regardless of quality.

There are, today, two routes to securing proper supplies. In reality, most elect for a combination but I shall maintain a seeming distinction. The first is through the capital city and its satellites. Any restaurateur worth his salt will notice that the French and francophile establishments of London and the Home Counties are in touch with far better suppliers than exist in corners of the provinces. They buy from big specialists, people who have large ethnic groups as customers for apparent rarities or luxuries; from shops that have been supplying the best to the richest for a very long time, thus can afford the demanding specifications of serious cooking – the grain-fed squab pigeon, the barbary duck; from wholesalers who have a direct line to the best suppliers in Paris, who import vegetables and fruit from Rungis; and from French dealers themselves, the most notable example of which is Maître Philippe Olivier, the cheesemonger of Boulogne, who supplies a score of the better restaurants of the south-east. A passable imitation of this method of buying can be constructed in the provinces. There are, for example, specialist suppliers that aim to deliver just this sort of merchandise on your doorstep – Vin Sullivan of Abergavenny is the most celebrated; or you can construct tenuous lines of supply from London itself – involving much meeting of trains, directing delivery drivers, sending friends with an empty car boot; or you can go yourself – a quick burst up the motorway on your day off. The result is interesting. It is now possible to consume the same duck, the same salad stuff, the same French beans and the same cheese from northern Scotland to the southernmost tip of France. Moreover, it is cooked according to the same recipes, dressed in the same oil, and tastes, more or less, identical. It is, very much, food after the last wave of French fashion.

The other way to buy is less reliable but has the advantage of offering foods that are unique to your district. You approach local merchants and growers and you take from them materials that you want. Meat is a perfect example. Loin of beef comes, *via* Smithfield, from Scotland. Fillet of beef is satisfactory from English beasts, so we can get it from our local butcher, Roy Shillabeer. Lamb we always get from Mr Luscombe, a Totnes butcher. He buys on the hoof in the market and we find his taste in carcases identical with ours. Mr Luscombe's pork, some of which he fattens himself, is also preferable to that of other butchers. Veal we tend to buy imported from Holland, it is both more tender and has a better taste. Chicken we have always liked to have grown and killed for us in a farmyard, although it has proved difficult to obtain it year in, year out. Ducks (usually Muscovies) are similarly grown and killed for us by a local farmer, as are rabbits and guinea fowl. The pattern, you can see, is complicated: nine different telephone calls, nine different cycles of growth and improvement. More variations can be worked on the same theme: young spring lambs may come from a rare-breeds farm, or from individual local farmers that are killing for themselves; hams from a farm that specialises in old pig varieties; kids from nearby goat-keepers. The same process may be described for vegetables. One grower specialises in garlic, one in courgettes, one in spinach; another is best for artichokes and asparagus.

Foolhardy would be the man who relies solely on this method of buying. There is, for instance, the terrible problem of the winter months. Thus a mongrel system is erected – lines are kept open to Covent Garden, wholesalers are kept sweet. It is not even invariably true that the local produce is the best, though it may be the freshest. What it does do, however, is ensure that the art of food production is not ignored in our pursuit of productivity and profit on the farm and that the restaurants of a locality serve food that is identifiably of that district. It is no longer easy in France to find the old dishes, the old regional cooking. It has long since been impossible in England. But without preciousness or quaintness, development of individual pro-ducers and growers may result in a heightened awareness of the richness of each region of England, though the Lord protect me from 'Sister Nonsense's Devonshire Syllabub' and dishes of that ilk.

The chapters which follow describe some of these suppliers and our relation with them. The monthly diaries sketch some of the broader problems that arise from the progress of the seasons. The recipes portray ways of dealing with the things once they arrive on the kitchen table. I, the author, act very much as a recorder. Much of the cooking was done by my partner, Joyce Molyneux, whose table you may still sample at the Carved Angel.

February

FEBRUARY DIARY

For once, Dartmouth seems the hub of the universe. This is the effect of having a company making a film of an Agatha Christie story, *Ordeal by Innocence*. Famous names spied wandering up and down the front; some even seen in the restaurant; convoys of vehicles transport men and cameras to the various locations; hotels are full; we keep running out of wine. It points up the difference between a restaurant in a conurbation with a constant flow of people and ourselves, stuck in a toytown (with many attractions) moribund for five months of the year. [1984]

Dartmouth is still delighting in the Christmas gift of butter from the EEC mountain. Initially, only the worst quality seemed available, so salted that it is impossible to eat. The allocation that has come to us from French producers, however, is excellent. There is much less of that greasiness that coats the mouth. Fresh (i.e. unsalted) butter is made in Devon by the dairy of Quicke Brothers at Newton St Cyres. Their pre-eminent achievement is a very good Cheddar cheese, but small amounts of butter are also made. Mr Riley, the dairy manager, tells me that they will usually freeze the unsalted butter because of the rancidity arising during storage. Fear of going off may be the reason for the heavy salt of most English butter, although the Scots do not seem to have this problem; it also allows the absorption of more water. I have never been sure whether English bread is underseasoned because all the salt is in the butter or whether butter needed to be heavily salted because the bakers could not make decent bread. For my own part, the combination of salted butter and sweet jams, honeys and marmalades is just about the nastiest thing that can be experienced. [1983]

Winter months are always times of using citrus fruits. We bought large boxes of Seville oranges to work through slowly, making bumper batches of marmalade. The new regulations for labelling do not make life any easier. Women's Institutes have been excluded by being a charity – I wish we were too. You now have to own a refractometer so as to inform the purchaser of the quantity of sugar in the finished article

Robin Congden of Sharpham Barton driving his flock of Friesland and Dorset Crosses to the evening milk.

(in percentage terms). You also have to state, more sensibly, the weight of fruit per pound in the original recipe. Estimating shelf life and its attendant problems are avoided if you can claim your product has a natural term of more than eighteen months, soon to be reduced to twelve.

Sevilles help for sauces such as *Maltaise* – a *hollandaise* with a bitter orange flavour. We also used them to marinate kid. A good recipe for an orange, carrot and onion *confit* has come from Alain Chapel's book *La cuisine est beaucoup plus que des recettes*. It goes well with terrines; we have served it with rissoles filled with game; it can accompany roast lamb. [1983]

The desertion of Dartmouth quays in the last months of bitter cold has not been a spur to more adventurous marketing. The fishermen have been loath to go out, particularly during a long spell of easterly winds which mean poor catches for the shellfish boats. When the weather is really bad, on every coast, the price of even the most humble species can go high. Monkfish reached the alarming level of £3 a pound on an especially bad day. There have been, however, some bright spots. We have seen prawns, there have been lobsters. When caught by inshore boats, the fish has been in good condition. We had a nice run of small school bass to vary the diet. [1983]

Reports have been heard of a crisis in the oyster fishery of the river Dart. The oysters are all Pacifics here. The trouble stems from the tin content of a certain anti-fouling paint used by boat and yacht owners. This causes the oysters to develop preternaturally thick shells, particularly at the hinge, and shrink to a minuscule size within. So little meat that they cannot be sold. In Europe, the legislators love their stomachs enough to ensure an immediate ban on this kind of paint. Here in England a statutory instrument is insufficient and we have to wait the ponderous enactment of a statute. As far as we are concerned, the crisis of more import is in stocks of native oysters. There is a parasite that attacks their blood cells and causes heavy mortality in summer months. You may have read of the difficulties experienced by the owners of the Duchy of Cornwall Oyster Farm on the Helford river. Macfisheries have decided to surrender their lease; Mr Hodges, the resident manager (whose family has been doing this for generations), is to take over. The only response to this disease is to clear the affected ground and leave it fallow for some time. The way, therefore, to maintain stocks in the short term is to take over more oyster beds to counter the higher rate of mortality. This he has been doing, or is planning to do. Simultaneously, he is experimenting with Pacifics and laying greater emphasis on his mussels and clams. The only comfort is that the parasite in question is harmless to human kind. [1984]

The difference in the positions of two of our major suppliers of vegetables reflects the problems encountered in running a farm on the one hand and a garden on the other. Mr Rogers has had seventy lambs born at Higher Week, but very little is happening to his vegetables. Although he has sown many of his seeds under glass, he has only planted out his parsley and his peas. The weather is still too cold to risk a whole crop when the requirements of his market are reliability and bulk rather than earliness at a high price. Admiral Haynes, however, is apparently more active because he makes a point of early crops. To attain this, he has to keep his glasshouse up to 14°C during some frosty windblown weeks. The Admiral hopes the courgettes will be earlier than ever this year because he has not repeated the mistake of watering them direct from the mains. This season they have been hand watered from a tank in the greenhouse to maintain temperature. He will plant out his potatoes in the first week in March – three rows of Ulster Sceptre, one of Sutton Foremost and two of Ulster Chieftain. For the first time he has used his own seed potatoes. There are also three rows of autumn-sown broad beans that should be ready for a June crop and two rows of garlic are being prepared to take as much advantage of the light as possible. [1981]

This may be the time of year when you look forward to produce from local growers but of course the wait is longer than you ever expect. Delay is made sweeter by the arrival of the seed catalogues. The usual result is a ludicrous and inflated order for seeds we shall never grow. Best solution is to give the packets to people with greener fingers. But the list is so enticing that something has to be done: sorrel, chervil, dill and green and bronze fennel for the herb garden. The sorrels are not only the French but also the Buckler Leaved, a ground cover plant with small leaves. I know that I cannot grow parsley; other herbs we usually buy in plant form. I am not so rash as to grow tarragon or basil, yet others manage it with the greatest of ease. For salads I have bought salad burnet, salad rocket, purslane and lambs' leaves. Purslane I find especially enjoyable. From a wide selection of Italian salad stuff now available in seed form in this country, I chose *misticanza* (*mesclain* in France), a cutting chicory *grumolo* which provides leaves during the summer and heads in the winter, a cutting lettuce *ricciolina da taglio*, another of the same type *a foglia liscia*, a red salad bowl lettuce from France and (a serious mistake this) a packet of witloof chicory. For the vegetable garden, an Italian spinach beet and some ornamental cabbages. For the hedgerow and stream, we have taken bergamot, anise hyssop, bistort, alexanders, yellow gentian, flax, wild white clover, evening primrose, pennyroyal and tuberous pea. You can see that the prospect of six months' happiness for 40p per packet is too much to resist. My normal failing is inadequate preparation – the fledgling plant, surrounded with weeds, is impossible to discern and eventually overtaken by its rampant competitors. [1984]

PIGEONS

'I mostly use young squab bred on corn, maize, imported from Bresse, as with all other poultry! . . . Sad isn't it.'
  Answer to my enquiring of a chef about the provenance of his pigeons, March 1985

'Young tame pigeons are much the finest eating, and should be caught as soon as they are a good size, fat, and pretty flush of feathers. As these birds are generally killed before they are brought to market, it will be necessary to observe whether they are stale or fresh; if stale, they will be green about the vent, and their eyes look changed. – Tame pigeons are mostly preferred to the wild. Wood pigeons are much larger than either wild or tame, but like them in other respects. The legs of old pigeons are large and red.'
  Family Cookery, 1812

For a country so devoted to dovecotes, we are surprisingly unenthusiastic about eating pigeons. While antiquarians have covered reams in catalogues of surviving buildings, a poulterer will pay little more than the cost of the cartridge for a bird. For all our affection, dovecotes remain untenanted. No longer do we harvest their nests. It was not always so; the great round buildings that adorn our parks and manors were common enough; so were the few nooks under the eaves of many a country barn; even church towers had their refuges. Their yield was high. The historian G. C. Coulton cites a Berkeley manor producing

2151 birds in a single year; Anne Wilson (*Food and Drink in Britain*, 1973) notes Dame Alice de Bryene's household eating pigeons on nearly every meat day through the summer; the monks of Pontoise (Coulton again) were able to take four cartloads of dung from their dovecote in one year, and a crop of 4500 birds as well. That the practice was socially divisive is well known; pigeons were the preserve of the manorial lord or the freeholder. Already, by the sixteenth century, the north country common man's fancy for the bird was well marked. One of the demands of the Pilgrimage of Grace in 1536 (a movement of reaction rather than revolution) was, 'That no man under the degree of knight or esquire keep a dove house, except that it hath been of an old ancient custom'. Anne Wilson postulates that in Roman Britain there may have been urban dovecotes, built on the pattern of Mediterranean terracotta additions to the roof. Many centuries later, Samuel Pepys wrote (30 June, 1660), 'Dined at home and Mr. Hawly with me upon six of my pigeons which my wife is resolved to kill here'. Is this a survival of a similar practice? However well attested the rearing and slaughter of pigeons, the skill seems to have died out. Perhaps the birds were too destructive of neighbours', and one's own, crops. Thomas Tusser admonishes that you must, whatever else, protect your peas. Consumption by wild birds and the consequent reprisals were perhaps adequate to supply the market. The development of other species and the greater productivity of agriculture may have caused the demand to lessen. Although they are eaten today, they do not have a high reputation – justifiably, too. It may be asserted that the reason for this is the decline in dovecotes. However, it should be noted that breeds that were esteemed for palatability, especially the Runts, did not have to live in dovecotes. Mrs Beeton reported people using rooms or lofts and observed that Runts were as happy in rabbit hutches as anywhere.

When I enquired about pigeons amongst my acquaintance, there was hardly a general acceptance of the species, let alone eagerness to use squabs bred in a dovecote (nowadays, a poultry shed). Some might even be said to have agreed with Morton Shand (*A Book of Food*, 1926): 'Ordinary pigeons, Bordeaux or otherwise, I abominate. It is said that the stomach can only digest one pigeon a month, which shows that many a man has a second palate in that organ of greater delicacy than that on which he prides himself.' His reference to 'Bordeaux pigeons' is to those birds that used, before the war, to be imported to the game dealers of England. They came with their gut in, but plucked; smothered, but not bled. They came graded: single crown, double

crown, treble crown. To return to my enquiries: the majority of
respondents used wild pigeons of one sort or another – bought locally,
taken from shoots in the neighbourhood, purchased (in West Country
establishments) from Vin Sullivan of Abergavenny. Wild pigeons are
also imported from France and are used by some chefs in preference to
English birds, probably because the selection is more rigid and knowledgeable. As one person wrote, 'My game dealer cannot guarantee the
tenderness of the meat'. Yet he should be able to tell the age from the
legs and the feathering.

Where wild pigeons are not used, the alternative is the squab. This is a
fledgling bird that has not flown. After it has taken wing, until the age of
six months when it begins to breed, it is termed a squeaker. Tom Stobart
(*Encyclopaedia of Cooking*, 1980) has a fine story of boys attaching
threads to the legs of nestling wood pigeons so they would not fly before
being collected for the table. Squabs normally fly at about four weeks.
Although a squeaker is an excellent feast, the muscular development
that occurs when they take to the air means that the flesh is neither so
succulent nor tender. It is difficult to credit but a squab, never having
moved from the nest, can manage to weigh 20 ounces after 24 days of
life. This weight is achieved by the Palmetto breed, an American bird,
that is now being reared in England. In France, they kill a little later in
life (according to one informant, although Alain Chapel says that they
should be between two and three weeks of age), and the size is smaller:
between 12 and 16 ounces in contrast to between 16 and 20. The flesh,
in both instances, is lighter than a wood pigeon's, in looks and taste.
That which we had in France I found somewhat insipid but meals of
English birds have produced verdicts of a definite pigeon flavour,
coupled with moistness and tenderness. The flavour seems more pronounced in the breast, especially close to the bone. The legs are small
and of little interest though not unpleasant. The skin is thick on these
British birds; although I had browned it well in a very hot oven, with a
stint on the open flame to begin, it was not crisp the whole way through.
The birds are plucked while still warm. They can be finished with a wax
dip. It would appear that the Chinese method is to scald them, lifting the
top layer of the epidermis. Whether this improves the crispness of the
roasted skin I cannot say; it should.

Pigeons are monogamous and couple for life. Their breeding habits
are consistent, even monotonous. They lay two eggs each time, replacing if one is taken away or lost. There are eighteen days to hatching.
Fertility is not an invariable 100 per cent. They start the cycle again

when the squabs have left the nest. Each pair, therefore, may yield up to 17 squabs per annum. Their conditions of captivity are small aviaries with nest boxes, constructed within large poultry sheds. They each hold about ten pairs. They may fly, but not extensively. It is important that the temperature be kept constant as they do not breed if it is too cold. Aristocratic French pigeons are fed corn, i.e. maize, but Richard Bradley (1732) advises tares (or vetch) or grains of 'inferior' corns, spurry or buckwheat, if you wish to increase their fertility. John Farley (1792) suggests hemp seed, to which they are very partial. English breeders are now using manufactured feeds rather than whole grains.

It is a moot point how long pigeons should be kept between death and consumption. Older books agree that squabs should be eaten within twenty four hours. After that their flavour, fugitive at the best of times, begins to disappear. Older and wild pigeons may be kept longer, but not above a day or two. However, modern chefs normally insist on squabs being hung a week. They should also, according to the English books, be gutted as soon as they are plucked. Bradley and Farley observe correctly that the pigeon has no gall; the liver may therefore be left in the bird if it is to be plain cooked. Eliza Acton thinks they have this organ, for she advises them to be drawn carefully for roasting. The English squabs of today have their gut left intact, though the crop is removed. However, the French *pigeonneau* comes eviscerated. A poulterer's comment is that the French birds, without gut, suffer far greater keeping problems than do the English. Actual importation is fraught with difficulties regarding the correct EEC definition of pigeons (as interpreted by HM Customs): game or poultry? Occasionally, time wasted in debate causes the birds stranded on the quayside to sour and thus need destruction. The practice here is for the birds to be killed then bled. This keeps the flesh light as well as, again, prolonging shelf-life.

David Carver of East Cornworthy, part of our parish, had buildings, formerly poultry sheds, that were vacant in 1985. He had been thinking about alternative commodities that might put them to some use and thus came across Stephen Noblett near Diss, Norfolk, the producer of Token Gold squabs from American Palmetto birds. Mr Carver has taken some breeding stock from this source and is now experimenting with their care. He must hope that restaurants in the region will be sufficiently interested to pay the price demanded, from £3 to £4 per bird. In weight terms, this is much less than the equivalent French import. Provided the birds taste as well, the home producers should be able to oust foreign competition. The price does not compare favourably to the wild pigeon at 65 to 75 pence. However, the two things are very different. The wild bird figures rarely on menus, and in our own home repertoire. For us, this is certainly due to their lack of reliability. Not only dry and tough, their flavour is strong, verging on the bitter. And the bitterness is not a pleasant one. Evidently, not all wild birds are like this, in which case they would *never* be consumed. However, the frequency of disappointment makes one wary. The squab will offer cooks reliability and size (one per person is ample), even if at a premium. It may be objected that encouragement of such a meat is a dilution of the taste of pigeon, comparable to the fashion for poussins in the fifties. One must admit its potential blandness – quail all over again – but the flavour of pigeon is there, in a delicate fashion well suited to balancing with complementary or contrasting sauces.

Casual encounter with a recipe for pigeons will raise the question of what sort of bird is specified. Earlier works will assume or dictate that the cook uses young birds; more recent ones will expect a purchase of wild pigeons of indeterminate age, with a pious hope that they are not old. Recipes for squabs are not frequent, especially in English books. The term was not applied to pigeons until 1694 (*OED*). While Charles Carter (1730) does specify squabs, distinguishing them from the 'young pigeons' used in other receipts, many other authors of the 17th to 19th centuries may have presumed that the pigeons were from the dovecote, whenever tenderness and youth were important. Question of type can be fairly important for timing of cooking. Squabs need much less, both in the pot and in the oven. Shona Crawford Poole, in a column in *The Times*, advises simmering pigeons for two hours *before* putting them into a suet crust for another two and a half hour boil. She simmers her pigeons for potting for three hours. It is partly a question of style. Alain Chapel, for his pot-au-feu of wood pigeons, boils them for twenty minutes, a time that would not be recommended by most English books for even the best quality wild birds. To me, the trouble with cooking them for so many hours as advised by sensible people, *i.e.* until they part from the bone with ease, is that they very nearly cease to be pigeon, or anything, save for an excessively strong and particular flavour. In defence of the long cookers, it should be said that many of the disappointments with pigeon come from being too ambitious, thinking that because they are small they will be cooked. They won't; they will just be tough.

On times for squabs, current English literature can seem adrift. *The Times* cook suggests roasting them for thirty to forty minutes at 220°C /

425°F, gas mark 7, and leaving them to rest for another ten minutes. James Beard has an interesting entry in his concordance to *Theory and Practice* (1977), 'The meat is darkish and flavourful . . . roast them in a baking dish with bacon over the breasts for 40 to 45 minutes at 200°C.' Twenty minutes at 225°C/430°F, gas mark 7, having first browned the breasts on top of the stove, then leaving to rest in the warm would appear to give a 450g bird a slightly pink hue to the flesh which yet comes away from the bone satisfactorily. Hannah Glasse would expect pigeons to take the same time as larks, that is, fifteen minutes.

An enormous number of pigeon recipes are rich and elaborate to an extreme. Carter, Glasse, Farley and others delight in stuffing them with rich forcemeats as well as using them in fishes where farce is used in place of a pastry crust, the famed pulpatoon or pupton. Many of these complications may be ascribed to the French, exemplified by this quotation of Hannah Glasse's receipt for pigeon pie:

Pigeon pie
Make a puff-paste crust, cover your dish, let your pigeons be very nicely picked and cleaned, season them with pepper and salt, and put a good piece of fine fresh butter with pepper and salt in the bellies; lay them in your pan, the necks, gizzards, livers, and pinions, and hearts lay between, with the yolk of a hard egg, a beef-stake in the middle; put as much water as will almost fill the dish, lay on the top-crust, and bake it well. This is the best way to make pigeon-pye; but the *French* fill the pigeons with a very high force-meat, and lay force-meat round the inside with ball [?forcemeat balls], asparagus-tops, and artichoke-bottoms, and mushrooms, truffles and morells, and season high; but that is according to different palates.

An entirely different tradition of pigeon cookery comes from inspection of Elisabeth Lambert Ortiz's *Book of Latin American Cooking* (1984) where, rather than combination with other meats, hard-boiled eggs and luxury vegetables which is one European hallmark, there can be found delectable braises with orange juice, peppers and wine or shrimps. The marriage with shrimps is echoed in an Alain Chapel recipe for squabs with a butter of freshwater crayfish. It does seem to work, indeed makes a worthwhile alternative to the more common chicken and crayfish. The South American way does seem to impart more zest than many of the older instructions. I give you here, however, two straightforward affairs. The first is from *Dumas On Food* (Davidson translation, 1978) and consists of a way with green peas that resembles the classic duck dish. It is a braise, therefore may be useful for wild birds of which you cannot guarantee the tenderness. The second is a simple roast, for use with squabs, that uses the flavour of citrus fruit.

Pigeon with peas

Remove the feathers from three or four pigeons and clean and gut them. Put the liver back in the empty cavity and tuck the feet inside. Leave the tips of the wings on the birds, but singe and clean them. Put a piece of butter in a casserole, brown the birds in this and then remove them.

You will already have cut some lightly salted belly pork into large dice, and soaked them for half an hour to remove the salt. Put them in the butter and brown, drain and remove before putting a good tablespoon of flour in the butter to make a little roux. This should be light in colour. Then put back the browned pork and the pigeons, and coat them in the roux. Add some bouillon little by little until you have a sauce-like consistency. Season with parsley and spring onions, half a bay leaf, half a clove of garlic and a clove of nutmeg. Put the casserole at the side of the stove so that the pigeons barely simmer.

When the cooking is half over, put in a litre of tiny peas and let them cook, taking care to stir them frequently. When they are cooked, taste and add salt if necessary. Skim off the fat; and remove the peas, so that you can reduce the sauce if it is too thin. Once the sauce has been reduced, arrange the pigeons and cover them with the mixture of peas and pork and serve.

Squabs with a mandarin and ginger sauce

You will need one squab of 450g per person. If you can find larger ones, of 500–525g, then half a bird may suffice, so long as the rest of the meal is reasonably substantial. Remove head, feet, winglets, neck and gut. Wipe out the interior. Make a stock with the trimmings, except for the liver.

Chop an onion and fry it in butter, adding in the chopped pigeon livers, seasoning and basil and marjoram. Share this between the cavities of the birds. Brown the seasoned birds in oil and butter on the top of the stove, flame them in brandy then roast them, basting once, for twenty minutes in an oven at 225°C / 430°F, gas mark 7. Reserve them while you make the sauce.

Grate half a teaspoonful of green ginger. Squeeze one mandarin orange. Wipe out the roasting pan of burnt onion pieces then deglaze with the small stock you have made. Reduce by at least two thirds, add a glass of white wine and continue to reduce. Put in the orange juice and ginger and adjust the seasoning with salt, pepper and a little sugar. Add double cream and reduce to the correct consistency. We served it with sweet corn, off the cob and seethed with cream.

It would be a brave cook who used wild pigeons for that recipe. However, it is possible to get away with them if you use the breasts alone, taking them off the carcase and cooking them in a pan, with a short roast at the end. This method works with surprising consistency for a salad of pigeon breasts as a first course. Having cooked the little breasts, you slice them extremely fine and join them to a salad dressed with some of the juices, oil or butter and lemon juice. Fine cutting overcomes any of the problems of toughness.

March

The month is one of waiting – waiting for customers to brave the weather, and for produce to grow or reach maturity. The euphoria of starting again is dissipated; the worries set in. [1982]

A survey reported this week in *The Catering Times* revealed that for 70 per cent of the population, the most important attribute of an eating place was cleanliness and hygiene. Only 58 per cent thought well-cooked or good food were more important. Perhaps the one flows from the other; nonetheless, the order seems wrong. [1983]

We have been offered the chance of produce direct from the Rungis market in Paris, via London. There are a number of restaurants, many of them French owned (but by no means all) that consistently draw the bulk of their supplies from France itself. One sympathises, much of the stuff is better in every way. One has also witnessed the considerable efforts that some of them have made to obtain fresh food from their immediate districts – ranging from persuasion of growers to advertising in the press for produce. [1982]

Mr and Mrs Harvey from Slapton have supplied early purple-sprouting broccoli, winter sown, that has proved a godsend. Their spinach beet has also been sending out youngish shoots that have proved tender and mild enough to eat. Because the leaves are rather large and there is a danger of toughness, we have been shredding them and sweating them in butter. This sort of spinach has a tendency to be like cold tea leaves if you cook it in a large batch to make a creamed spinach. [1982]

Mr J. Distin has been doing well with prawns. He has lifted his prawn pots and baited about twenty lobster pots which he is planting singly in good locations. They have paid him dividends – he brought in thirty pounds weight in the first week in March. Robert Dart, meanwhile, has lifted his pots and is concentrating on scallops. His yields have been

Newton Abbot market.

high, their condition excellent. Surprisingly, the beds he has been dredging have been very close to Dartmouth; we expected them to have been worked out ere this. Thus, in Lyme Bay, a subscriber recalled that in his youth, before the Second World War, there were several boats that put out from Budleigh Salterton to take herring. Their disappearance from those waters (herring are liable to sudden and unexpected changes in distribution) was ascribed to over-exploitation of the scallop beds and the consequent change in marine ecology. Likewise, nearer to home, the queen, a small scallop of sweet flavour, has entirely disappeared through over-dredging in the last fifteen years.

Some flat fish, Dover sole for instance, is full of roe at present. Lemon soles are through their worst, as is plaice. Turbot and brill continue in good heart. This is the time of year for chicken turbot and brill. They cost nearly £1 a pound less than the adult fish but still make very good eating – firmer fleshed and better flavour than a lemon sole (which costs almost as much). Inshore cod has been quite wonderful. One is occasionally shamed at our insistence on 'noble' fish after eating a lunch of grilled fillet of cod. It does need to be fresh, however. As it stales, the flesh begins to fall apart in gaping slashes. It dries out. It becomes boring and, then, unpleasant. The best is therefore caught by inshore boats who can get it to market without extended chilling in the well of the deck. This fish is not usually so large as the deep sea quarry of the northern waters, but one is prepared to forgo some of the flavour that comes from age, cold water and slow growth for the sake of freshness. Another cheap fish that proved first rate was a very large (50lb) conger eel. Normally, conger is palatable but has a tendency to dryness, to be rather tough or fibrous, and to have only a moderate flavour. Never try cooking or eating the tail – that part below the vent. The bone structure is so complex that it is virtually impossible to extract the flesh. However, like monkfish, the larger the specimen, the better the meal. The flesh had a texture and translucence that was entrancing. [1984]

HANNAFORD'S OF TORCROSS, BUTCHERS

Hannaford's are family butchers in the small village of Torcross at the southern end of Slapton Sands, some five miles down the coast from Dartmouth. Their business practices are particularly interesting as an example of a genuine butcher, i.e. one who in some instances fattens, certainly kills and then sells. Too many butchers, even when they have the air of being totally competent, may do no more than take the meat off the lorry from the wholesalers, with no more care for the finer points of its condition than an ironmonger. Hannaford's still chooses the meat on the hoof, certainly with the lamb and beef. It is sometimes possible that your meat will come better from a large supermarket chain with skilled buyers working to high standards than from a small individual butcher with no room for hanging and no clout with the wholesaler.

Our meat supplies are drawn from three main sources. There is the large wholesaler in Exeter, Russell, dependent on Smithfield for Scotch beef and Dutch veal; we use them for loins and ribs of beef, some mutton and, increasingly, for veal. There is Luscombe of Totnes from whom we obtain the bulk of our English lamb and some pork. And there is Shillabeer in Dartmouth who supplies us with chicken, guinea fowl, English beef fillet, oxtail and bones. None of these has their own slaughterhouse, although Russells do have links within their company with their abattoir in Aberdeen. The rest of our meat comes from a variety of people: Heal Farm brings young lambs from old breeds, venison and some pork products; Mrs Wall supplies us with kid; Sebastian Lange sometimes has sheep killed; geese come from Mrs Reeves or Mr Cudd. Farmers, needing an animal killed for their own consumption, can call on the services of an itinerant slaughterman who lives in Dartmouth. They are not, however, allowed to sell this meat. If they wish to sell, they must take it to the abattoir at Newton Abbot. Hannaford's are one of two butchers that have their own registered slaughterhouse in this district.

There was an abattoir in Dartmouth itself until shortly after the war. The premises survive, on a site quaintly known as Jawbones, occupied by the fishmonger, a welding concern and a builders' supplier. One of the better documents of recent Dartmouth history is a report on the public health and sanitation of the town compiled for the Local Government Board by Dr F. St George Mivart in 1914. There had been outbreaks of scarlet fever among townspeople, alarming the authorities at the Naval College. This prompted an investigation of local government effectiveness by central government. Mivart's comments on abattoirs and food suppliers are worth repeating here, to put our own conditions into some sort of perspective.

There are four private slaughterhouses which I am assured are registered though the register had at the time of my visit been mislaid; there is also a public abattoir. All these places are far removed from houses and have been placed near a locality known as 'Jawbone' on the hill to the south-west of the town at an altitude of about 500' above O.D. The condition of these places calls for no special comment save that an enormous accumulation of blood and offal was found at one slaughterhouse and at another the overflow of blood and filth soaking down the hill is, as Mr Hill's report indicates, dangerous to a source of public water supply.

The public slaughterhouse erected is a brick building constructed in three sections so that it can be used by three butchers, but at present only one section is in use. For some reason the place is not popular; two owners of private slaughterhouses allow the use of their premises by other butchers. The floors of the killing rooms are apparently porous rough brick forming a bad surface for cleansing. The abattoir is only about 90 yards from the isolation hospital building. At the time of my visit there was a large accumulation of blood, filth, and slaughterhouse refuse on the ground only about 60 yards from the well giving a supply of drinking water to this hospital . . .

There are twenty registered milk dealers, of whom 12 are said to keep cows, and most of their premises were visited. At my first visit to Dartmouth I found that no alteration had been made in the milk dealers' register since 1898, but the book has since been brought up to date. Some of the milk vendors' premises in the town are mere general shops – even drapery goods being sold there. I found pans of milk standing without protection from dust and flies. Some of the shops were dirty and the means of scalding milk vessels seemed insufficient.

The cow-keepers' premises, of which I visited nearly all, were found extremely defective. Cow-houses almost without exception were filthy; some were in a disgusting condition and seemed not to have been whitewashed for an indefinite period. Low-pitched, dark, and wanting in ventilation, some of them smelt offensively. Floors, everywhere of rough and uneven surface, were dirty and often thickly coated with dung. At nearly every farm there was a large manure heap close to the doors and windows of the cow-houses, and at one farm the accumulation was so great as almost to block the entrance. At another farm the hands of a milker just about to commence work were found dirty. With dairies there was much less fault to find. The majority of them were cleanly though too often used as a store for miscellaneous articles of food and household effects; some dairies communicate directly with dwelling house rooms.

There was an old register of bakehouses, but it had not been kept up for years. The inspector of nuisances was not in a position to say how many bakehouses there are in the town, but there seemed to be a considerable number. While a few of those visited were clean, the majority were very dirty and ill-kept; some, indeed, were in a disgraceful condition. Many of the premises are in no way suited for this trade. The buildings are not only old and dilapidated, but also wanting in light and ventilation; in some instances the ceilings, walls and floors are so broken and defective that cleanliness is almost impossible. In some bakehouses there are large rambling lofts overhead and running back into the rock. Some of these were found full of miscellaneous effects and rubbish, the ceiling festooned with cobwebs and in some cases harbouring bats. In two of the lofts I found household linen drying, and in one of them, in addition to household linen, was a store of flour, insufficiently protected from dirt. In three instances I found hand-flushed hopper closets in filthy condition close to the bakehouse door; one of these closets had to serve three families.

I found in a dark room adjoining one bakehouse, in open sacks and boxes, a quantity of flour which was covered with dirt. A large collection of rat traps were hanging conspicuously in the bakehouse. The manager admitted that the place is overrun with rats, as are also, I believe, most of the old bakehouses of Dartmouth.

The response of the Town Council and the community at large to this blistering comment on their public health was disbelief and denials. There was some improvement in administration and the keeping of registers but it left the surface of life largely unruffled. So have most criticisms in the last hundred years. I am mindful of its piquant descriptions while reading about Hannaford's improvements to their own slaughterhouse to bring it up to E E C standards. It throws into relief the whole question of diet and health today. We are told, with some reason, of the pernicious effects of white flour, white sugar, heavy metal pollution and food additives; the diet and mode of life of previous generations are held up as a paradigm. This they certainly are not, on the score of either environmental pollution or food additives. This does not affect the absolute truth of those who would improve our present state, but it does alter our perspective of relative decline or betterment.

The shop at Torcross was founded by Mr Hannaford's grandfather, who came to the village in 1890. He rented the fields at the back of the shop, in which is now found the slaughterhouse, and kept geese, chickens and ducks there. Sufficient business was found by delivering with a horse and cart to all the villages around – Hallsands, down the coast, and as far as East Prawle. At that time there was a butcher in Slapton village, now the most important sector of the custom. Until the installation of electricity in 1935, the keeping of meat was a constant problem, in the shop and on the slow country round. Ice was imported by carter from Brixham, where it was manufactured for the fishing industry. Electricity enabled them to put in a cold room which has served them, with only a new motor, to the present day. The round of the neighbouring villages is still essential to the business and accounts for three-quarters of all the meat sold.

The Hannafords buy direct from farmers rather than go to market. This may change in future as the collection of subsidies by the farmer necessitates his stock going through the market to qualify. Market arrangements are currently unsatisfactory for the conduct of daily business. The market at Kingsbridge is not a very good one, which means going to Newton Abbot and a large increase in transport costs. The market has also changed to an inconvenient day for them. When buying at market, the animals arrive late in the afternoon and have to be kept overnight before killing. There are not the facilities at Torcross for this accommodation, so they prefer to kill on the day of arrival from a farm, after the animal has had time to settle.

Only beef and lamb are bought in this way. Pigs used to be, but the bacon factory at Totnes, run by Harris's, has contracted with most local farmers for their supplies so that it is not easy to buy pigs individually. Pork comes from the North Devon Meat Company. They used to buy from Nortons of Plymouth. However, the sales manager left to go to NDM and the Hannafords followed him, on the grounds that he knew best what they wanted.

I have heard tales of Mr Hannaford appraising a farmer's beef – how he will tour the field picking out the beasts, assessing their conformation on the hoof, observing that some have run on too hilly ground which will make them too tough, timing their delivery for optimum condition and yield. He will buy most of the British breeds: South Devons, Herefords crossed with Friesians, Ayrshires (which he says are the best for veal), but does not like the foreign strains, Limousins or Charolais. Best for supermarkets with too much lean and too much muscle – comments which we make ourselves when eating beef in France and, broadly, the same opinion as Mr Wright of Russell's when extolling the virtues of Scotch beef. In former years, a beast might be three years old to reach its best condition; this has now changed and twenty months is the normal age of purchase. If beef has come down in age, largely through changes in feeding and breeding, so has the sale of veal disappeared. There was a time when one or two calves were killed every week but the alteration of subsidy, increasing the amount on prime beef, caused that supply to dry up.

As Hannaford's are complete butchers, they have the ability to supply all sorts of offal. Ox cheek they used to make into pies, but now it goes to the district's dogs. Tripe and other offal have increased their sale – the former to people who retire from the North, and to tourists – Devonians don't eat tripe.

While beef comes from a number of farmers, perhaps half a dozen, sheep and lambs come predominantly from one, although the winter sees a large sale of New Zealand. There are breeds of sheep that give better conformation, as of beef. Dorsets and Hampshires give too much fat for present tastes, so the bulk are Suffolk crosses put to South Devons or Border Leicesters. Suffolk crosses give better milk which ensures a healthier start for the lambs – they also have a high number of twins and triplets. Mutton doesn't sell any more, though farmers send it to the Midlands, presumably for the Asian market. Every week, they may kill 3 beef and 20 lambs as well as taking 8 pigs and dealing with at least 50 chickens. This creates a lot of waste, much of which is taken away for pet meat. Some of it (partly digested food for instance) makes good garden fertiliser. Hides are a useful by-product, improving in quality as the use of barbed wire goes down and as warble fly, which left holes along the spine, is eradicated. The hides are exported to Spain.

In the slaughterhouse, animals are treated one at a time, each being bled and half-skinned before the next is brought in. Carcases are left to cool in the ambient temperature – there is no attempt to cool artificially. The scale of business decrees a relatively short time before the meat is offered for sale. In the summer this will be about two days, in the winter a week. However, a rib that we had recently from Hannaford's was two weeks old – beautifully tender.

Although in the country and not a monster affair, the slaughtered beasts still have to be inspected and authorised by the local authority. This must be one reason for there being some unwillingness to see a proliferation of small abattoirs. The Hannaford record is good; very few infected animals, perhaps two, in the course of a long working life. Reg Hannaford, when questioned about his clean bill, points out that he doesn't make a practice of buying diseased stock, another indication of his skill at selecting on the hoof.

Sausages are made at the shop, two hundredweight a week and more in the summer. Regulations decree that they should have 37 per cent meat content. Hannaford's have 85 per cent and upwards, with no preservatives. It is interesting to note that variations in sales will be caused by such things as a large mackerel catch at Beesands, ruining their calculations for a week. In sausages, like so many other things, tastes have changed. Only half the amount of pepper is used to former recipes and still people say they are too hot. Mr Hannaford admits that in the old days the pepper was there not only because people liked it but also to disguise the state of the meat in hot summer months. The same change, as we have all noticed, is seen in fat. There was a time when they would sell one inch layers of fat cut from the joints of pork to 'old timers' to fry for their breakfasts.

To say that people like the Hannafords are a dying breed is wrong. Reducing they may be, but there are still butchers in this district, as in many others, although predominantly in the country, who choose their meat with equal skill and discrimination. There may be vast zones that are served only by Dewhursts and the Argentine, but this is often the fault of the customer. Some of the Hannafords' comments make one realise how much our eating habits are influenced by purely financial and governmental considerations, subsidies and regulations. I am sure that no civil servant ever thinks of the gustatory effect of his actions.

April

The Lloyds of Dittisham Fruit Farm called by with a report of their preparations for this year and comments on the past season. They observed how vegetable growers were suffering in general, citing the recent difficulties of firms at Lea Valley in London and Elburton near Plymouth. The Lloyds are expanding their vineyards by 20 per cent this year. Their fruit cordials have also proved themselves. Their blackcurrant of 1984 was very satisfactory. Half a ton of fruit went to make 50 gallons. More work has gone into choosing strawberry varieties that are suited to our climate. Saladin, Tantalon and Haphill are the new types; the latter being a specific replacement for Cambridge Favourite. They have also planted Leo raspberries, a late variety that has proved less virus-prone than Glen Cova. Space devoted to loganberries was doubled last year and a similar expansion is to be accorded tayberries this year. Desirée and Pentland Javelin potatoes were planted out in mid-March, taking advantage of the warm spell we had then. On the peas and beans, they are no longer growing runners, but continuing with French beans and stick beans – a shorter plant with a flat podded bean like a small runner. They have tried some French broad bean seeds as well as English. Hurst Green Shaft (a second early) is the variety of garden pea that they find best; they will also be growing mange-tout and sugar peas. They are continuing to raise outdoor cherry tomatoes – Alfresco and Gardener's Delight – the seeds were sown in the last week of March.

Winter brought its problems. The artichokes seem to have suffered badly from the extreme frost. The spinach that was over-wintered was destroyed in one gulp from a flock of sheep. Although they operate on a small scale, the Lloyds are careful of their land. One might assume that they would go for continual cropping, aided by the resources of ICI. Not at all; two fifths of their ground is occupied by permanent plantings – vines and such. The remainder is rotated, lying fallow in the time-honoured manner. [1985]

There have been a lot of Israeli strawberries (better than the Spanish) and New Zealand raspberries. We are unsure of the variety of the latter but they come to us in very good condition with a not unpleasant flavour (something of the loganberry in them). If one accepts the shortcomings of these imported fruits, they do make a welcome change. Kumquats have also been sent us – rather later in the year than we expected. They have been delicious, particularly with a meringue made with the zest of orange, filled with a honey ice cream, topped with a kumquat sauce made by boiling the sliced fruit (minus the pips) in a syrup of a pint of water to half a pound of sugar, then whizzing it in the blender and stabilising it with a little cornflour. As an accompaniment, sliced kumquats are poached until tender in another syrup. [1983]

At sea the month has been mixed. Scallops have been of the best quality; lobsters sometimes plentiful but increased in price – Easter demand and lack of working time on the part of the fishermen; crabs scarce but good. Turbot and brill are in better condition than ever and plentiful. Dover soles have started to carry too much roe. The salmon season started gently. The Tamar has also seen a poor beginning. We had a good twelve pounder and three trout during the first week. People were at first reluctant to buy, perhaps thinking it had been farmed. Although the fish have been in good condition they have been pale in colour. This is a phenomenon that occurred last year. One fisherman said that it was due to their not having eaten enough prawns on their way to the river and that you can tell if it was going to be a pale fish by certain (undisclosed) characteristics of the head. The start of the season has also set off a debate in the kitchen that will doubtless rumble on through the summer. If the fish is used too soon after landing, the effect of *rigor mortis* is a retraction and a buckling of the flesh when cut and, perhaps, a slight toughness when eaten. The problem is gauging the correct length of time to leave it. One fish was still behaving in this manner after three days in the fridge. [1982]

Newton St Cyres Cheddar has been obtainable in first rate condition and we have been enjoying a blue Cheshire from the new cheese shop in Dartmouth. Although we may join in the chorus of regret for the passing of former farmhouse glories, the present position seems much healthier than it has been for a long time. In 1937, Edward Bunyard wrote in *The Epicure's Companion* that Cheddar, 'I am reliably informed, may and does reach the supreme, but I can only say that so far

David Lloyd of Dittisham Fruit Farm training his loganberries.

it has never come my way, and thus gives me yet another reason for looking forward to the morrow.' Osbert Burdett had the good fortune to taste the real thing but, reading between the lines in his *Little Book of Cheese* (1933), one feels that neither of these authors had the opportunities now offered to us by the right shops. Pasteurisation may be a commonplace, but some general rise in standards amongst the atrocities may be detected. [1983]

DITTISHAM FRUIT FARM

Seasons of the year seem often to be there for the flouting. The pleasure of imported fruit and vegetables, bringing summer to a winter scene, is a harmless one, if not carried to extremes. One is prepared to accept a diminution of flavour on grounds that would not be allowed a home grower. We hope for English strawberries, from the vale of Taunton or the Cornish side of the Tamar, in time for Easter each year. However, these are hot-house grown and have rarely had the benefit of the sun. Their flavour, too, leaves much to be desired. For the decent open field crops, we rely on David and Ingrid Lloyd at Dittisham Fruit Farm. Here, two miles inland from Dartmouth, they have twenty-two acres. Strawberries occupy eight acres, raspberries one and vines are grown on a half acre plot. The remainder of the land is under a variety of vegetable and root crops, currants, gooseberries, loganberries and tayberries. Nothing is grown under glass or plastic, so all depends on the weather and the skills of horticulture. There is no doubt that the Lloyds exercise considerable vigour and care in raising their crops which have their effect on yield and quality, the weather notwithstanding.

The Lloyds have been farming here since 1977 and in even this short span have seen considerable change in the market. They do not employ permanent help, thus depend on the pick-your-own system to realise the cash value of the bulk of their crop. However, they supply local restaurants and some shops and will ship large surpluses off to the bigger wholesalers. Students provide a few picking hands during the season.

For strawberry growers, a major bugbear is competition from imports. As the Mediterranean countries improve their production, especially by selecting better varieties and developing better means of transport and preservation (at whatever cost to our health), so our cost in fuel and tillage of achieving early crops of soft fruit rises out of proportion. Soon, the English farms will thus be restricted to supplying the high season trade. This, of course, earns less money. One saving grace is that the best-flavoured varieties, for example Cambridge Vigour, travel badly. Thus we will always have to rely on home-grown produce for the very best in taste.

Competition from abroad, combined with the relatively low price of agricultural produce, has left David Lloyd disenchanted with the possibilities of large scale production of greenstuffs such as beans or peas. A margin of profit does not appear until the acreage is far above that available to him. Success may come from the short-range supply of specific varieties and luxury items. This is how his trade has developed with Dartmouth restaurants and shops since we have known him. Potatoes: ultra-small Pentland Javelins for earlies, Desirées for main-crop (also especially small if requested); spinach: particularly Medina, a small and delicate flavoured leaf; mange-tout peas: seeds from France, and sugar peas; garden peas; asparagus; artichokes: Vert de Laon and a Tuscan variety with a small head, spiky leaves and purple colour; lettuce and chicories: a range of varieties, using French and Italian seeds; beans; tomatoes: outdoor cherry tomatoes and large tomatoes such as Marmande; and herbs: basil, dill, coriander, parsley, chervil. The produce is invariably fresh and we have a degree of choice in time of picking and, from year to year, of variety and species. Dealing with growers like the Lloyds has too the excitement that buying imports through wholesalers can never have – beating the weather, savouring the new season's crop, moving from one thing to another as the months pass. The unpredictability has its trials too. There was a dinner for which we specified Dittisham asparagus, the first of the springtime. However, the heavens opened and the frosts struck, growth was retarded and we managed three tiny spears per person. Embarrassment was compounded by my overcooking the whole lot.

The Fruit Farm may attain a crop of fifteen tons of strawberries and a ton of raspberries. Added to that they are increasing their yields of loganberries and tayberries and have large quantities of black and red currants and dessert gooseberries. Their situation in the relatively moist climate of the south west causes some of their yields to be lower than in other fruit-growing areas. Thus Cambridge Favourites produce five to eight times as much in the eastern parts of the country. The Lloyds need to try newer varieties, for example (in 1985) Saladin, Tantalon and Haphill, to compensate for these problems. The trouble with these, as with so much in vegetable and fruit production, is that extraneous requirements lead to a change in taste and texture. I had to mount a demonstration of strawberry varieties away from Dartmouth and was warned that Cambridge Vigour, the most esteemed for flavour and balance, would not travel well. The event proved the admonition. They bruised badly in the bumpy transport and had lost their zest by the time the tasting began. The newer sorts, normally looked upon with disdain, are more successful. But this does not detract from the Vigour's quality in ideal conditions. The moral is to buy locally, picked fresh. Early on a summer's day, we tried several of the types picked by the Lloyds. This was the result of our tasting:

Cambridge Vigour: a constant winner which grows well here. Medium-sized berries, palish flesh, intense flavour with excellent balance.

Red Gauntlet: surprised us by its high rating. A large fruit with pale flesh, not very sweet but good flavour.

Tamella: a new variety with red flesh and large fruits. Very juicy but sharp.

Cambridge Favourite: medium-sized, pale-fleshed. Lacking acidity and with little flavour to give it bounce.

Gorella: a small fruit with very red flesh. Again low on acidity; this is the boring variety that is often grown in Mediterranean fields for out-of-season exports.

Tanella: another new variety, a large fruit, sharp taste.

As strawberries, so raspberries have their varieties and their climactic pros and cons. The later season is the best for flavour and depth in Devon, the time they match the best of the Scottish lowlands, with Malling Admiral as a late summer fruit and Zeva (a variety from Switzerland) for the autumn. Assaults from virus disease have been prolonged on raspberry varieties so that most of the old sorts have been replaced by scientifically reared virus-free strains, particularly at the East Malling Research Station. It is still a problem in South Devon, perhaps because of its wet climate; so, during 1984/5, the Lloyds have been replacing their Glen Cova (the principal mid-season variety) with virus resistant Malling Leo. The warmth of the region, however, means that crops are harvested long into the autumn, though with a diminution of flavour as the sun reduces its span. We have had them coming to us as late as November.

The intention at Dittisham Fruit Farm is to maximise profit potential with soft fruit as well as green vegetables. This takes some surprising turns because the Lloyds have a limited amount of land. Their chief enterprise with the strawberries, raspberries and black currants is to make a cordial of each fruit using the surplus crops at the end of the season. I give here their recipe for raspberries, together with comments on the practice of Michel and Maggie Beaugeard, restaurateur friends of ours in Normandy, who also make their own raspberry liqueur.

Raspberry cordials
Take the fruit from the ripest autumn crop. Leave them to attain maximum darkness and juiciness before actual mould growth sets in. Prepare a sugar syrup at a strength of two ounces of sugar in a cup of water (per pound of fruit). Dissolve the sugar over the heat and, when it is cool, add it to the raspberries. Mix and grind the fruit with your hands in a large bowl. Put the resulting pulp in a jelly bag or a hair sieve to drip overnight. When you have extracted the last ounce of liquid, measure the result and add alcohol in the correct proportion. The Lloyds use 100 per cent grain spirit, so achieve a 25 per cent alcohol content by adding one quarter of the volume of raspberry juice in spirit. The same effect may be achieved by adding vodka but brandy, Armagnac or Calvados could be used. The amount you add depends on their strength (it is a simple mathematical calculation) but your goal is 25 per cent alcohol content so that the fruit may be satisfactorily preserved.

Once the mixture is made it should be put in jars that can be well sealed and left to mature for at least three months in a cellar or cool dark room before bottling. David Lloyd points out that if you are unlucky there will be too much pectin in the fruit and it will cause your mixture to set. 'Once you end up with jelly and strings, you've had it.' It is thus wise to ensure that all your fruit is very ripe indeed.

The French version uses more sugar and, because they are making for their own consumption, their quantities are less precise. Michel Beaugeard takes the autumn crop and puts it into a large and sealable container. He adds an equal weight of sugar and mixes the sugar and fruit to a pulp with his hands; then a roughly equal amount of spirit (in his case Calvados). This is then left in the container in a warm, not cool as in England, place for three months. The bottle we tasted had come from one that had been left for twelve months. When you can wait no longer, put the pulp through the fine plate of a food mill and leave to strain through a muslin or jelly bag. If the pulp is too thick to strain easily, you can let it down with some water. Taste the end result and add either water, if it is too alcoholic and fiery; sugar, if it is too tart; or alcohol, if it is too weak. He, too, stresses the need for a strength of about 25 per cent if you wish your liqueur to have a long life.

At the same time as they sent their recipe for raspberries, the Beaugeards mentioned their *griottes* or morello cherries in Calvados. We have brought back *quesches* and *mirabelles* for treating in like manner from an autumn visit to Caen. However, our success was moderate, the plums lacked the strength of flavour to come through the spirit.

Cherries in brandy

Take your cherries and reduce their stalks to half an inch in length. Prick each fruit two or three times with a needle. Put the fruit in a plastic bucket, cover it with Calvados, seal with plastic film and a lid. Leave in a warm place for about three months. At this juncture, add about half the original weight of the cherries in sugar, stir to dissolve and replace the covers. Leave for another six months. Since one is not usually doing enough for an army, it is probably most sensible to make these in sweet jars or Parfait jars, with useful informative labels about weights and dates. Don't use the boring dessert cherries that are often the only thing you can buy in English shops.

May

One result of an unhealthy emphasis on the art rather than the fact of food has been to make restaurant meals less digestible than domestic ones. There is a constant pressure to elaborate or enrich, no matter whether the chef subscribes to the tenets of *nouvelle cuisine*. Four out of five meals in restaurants leave me half dead for twelve hours. I have never understood why. It is neither food poisoning nor excessive alcohol. My appetite, at home, is gargantuan. Yet, if the same approach is followed at restaurants, nemesis will follow. It often seems that a meal purchased without subsequent bodily distress is a greater achievement than a meal whose elements show the highest artfulness. It may come down to habit; the cause no more than the aggregate of the ingredients, the dissimilarity with one's daily fare and the stress of the occasion itself. [1983]

Admiral Haynes has made his first pickings of courgettes. A little later than last year for he has reduced the winter heat in the greenhouse. This will delay some of the other crops, notably basil and tomatoes. The extremely wet March delayed the potatoes, helped little by the succeeding drought, then near frosts. However, Admiral Haynes had put in his Ulster Sceptres which we feel to be the best thing in our potato year. The first Cornish new potatoes were reported from Helford at the beginning of the month and were with us by the 10th. The price of Jerseys has been so excessive that we welcomed the English product for economic as well as chauvinist and stomachic reasons. [1982]

You will have noticed that the weather has been worse than ever before. It becomes tedious to report yet another tempest, a bigger flood, a wilder wind. The result is that the season has been delayed. Asparagus is running at least a fortnight behind last year. Strawberries are equally late. There are few signs yet of courgettes from Admiral Haynes; generally we are having to rely on more imports than we would like. Mr Rogers has few crops nearing readiness but does report hope for the

early summer. His new potatoes are making good progress – he has planted Ulster Sceptre and Maris Bard. For his maincrop, he has selected Pentland Hawk rather than Pentland Ivory. He was observing the other day how necessary it is that growers should dust their crops to inhibit sprouting in the clamp. Some Desirée potatoes that he has had to buy in have not been so treated and show signs of poor keeping. [1983]

One pleasant arrival has been sea spinach. This grows wild on the cliff tops on Stoke Fleming. The leaves are fleshy. When picked young they can be used in salad but they quickly become too tough for this. The taste is tangy, as if the salt has got inside. When cooked with a little butter, it makes an excellent vegetable or a small accompaniment to scallops or some other fish. [1981]

I have been talking to Mike Lynn about his work on board Dartmouth's only trawler, a small boat that Mike runs on his own, or with one boy to help. A good day's fishing will consist of three hauls, the total time, from departure to return to port, being thirteen hours. He normally fishes between five and ten miles off shore. He has to know his ground for he cannot afford to let his trawl be damaged on a wreck or on rocks. Nor can he linger over unproductive areas. The hauls will each take between two and three hours. When complete, the trawl is hoisted inboard, emptied, made ready and cast into the sea immediately. The yield is expressed in baskets, each weighing about four and a half stone. On the day we talked, Mike had been able to make only two hauls. On the first he caught a basket of lemon soles and a basket of mixed flats – dabs, plaice and the like. The second was more successful – he got a basket of flats, a slack basket of lemons, a basket of cuttlefish, two dozen scallops, a stone of monkfish and a basket of gurnard and horse mackerel. Much of this fish has to be gutted and sorted before landing at Kingswear quay whence it is driven to Brixham market. Mike is a member of the Brixham co-operative of fishermen. He is thus bound to send the bulk of his catch through his own market-place. [1983]

The east wind gives trouble to the fishing boats and changes the behaviour of their prey. Yields at Brixham have not been great. Many trawlers have transferred their attentions to scallops. Discovery of new beds off Portland has been giving them enormous catches with a guaranteed sale to the shellfish processors. Their landings are so large that the price has dropped, making it difficult for small boats such as

Crabbers tied up at Kingswear quay. Dartmouth is in the background.

Robert Dart's to make enough to cover their costs. The greater efficiency of modern fishing is a worrying thing. One boat discovers a good patch and suddenly it is worked out. So much is brought in (each boat taking several thousand dozen) that it can be used only for frozen food. The results for the sea bed will take years to correct. [1984]

This month saw the arrival of half a carcase of a Simmenthal-Friesian cross heifer from Sebastian Lange at Coomery, Tuckenhay. The animal had been barley fed and spent much of its life indoors. Joyce Molyneux reminded me of the fashion for barley beef some years ago. This was much in the same tradition; there was not much fat, very little marbling (except in the topside) and the colour was pale with a close texture. Although some of the joints were tender, for instance the fore-ribs, others, such as the topside, were firmer than expected. We hung the meat for nearly two weeks. The flavour was not strong. The meat that required slow cooking for tenderness lacked the taste necessary to carry a steak and kidney pudding or beef *bourguignon*. There were many pleasures from this beast, not least the small rib steaks and the brined silverside which made wonderful eating.

The weights of the various joints were as follows:

total weight of the half beast, before boning or butchery: 200lbs

trimmed forequarter meat, for stewing	37lb
fillet	3.5lb
entrecôte (on the bone)	12.25lb
rump	13.25lb
foreribs (on the bone)	11lb
silverside	8.25lb
topside	10.5lb
thick flank	6.5lb
trimmings off the hindquarter	6.5lb
	108.75lb

[1982]

Another enjoyable purchase from Brixham was a tuna. These are very rarely landed here. For some reason, the boat came north instead of going to Spain. We bought a ten-pound fish. Others were being shunted around the quay on fork-lift trucks, they were so large. Like an overgrown mackerel, we cooked it with white wine and served it cold, with a pimento salad and a herb mayonnaise. Dense in texture, perhaps not adequately bled, it made quite good eating. On the same day we took some weavers, again an uncommon offering from the market. This is a fish that I enjoy for its firmness and taste. [1983]

A high spot in eating has been a leg of lamb that came with Colin and Sue Kellam unexpectedly one evening. The lamb from whence it came was only two months old. We roasted it plainly, spiked with garlic. Coupled with their first asparagus and radishes and a bottle of Chambolle-Musigny 1969 from Lionel Bruck, it made a pleasant hour. [1984]

FISHING IN STOKENHAM

The manor and village of Stokenham, some five miles down the coast from Dartmouth, takes in the whole of Start Point and the lower end of Slapton Sands. As with so many parishes of the South Hams, it contains several outlying hamlets that led more or less independent existences. The Elizabethan court rolls of the manor relate to twenty-eight constituent settlements. Their fortunes varied over the centuries; many have shrunk to a single farm; others became villages in their own right, with perhaps a chapel (albeit dissenting); and some were swept away by catastrophe (the ruin of Hallsands after its erosion due to the removal of shingle at the end of the last century) or by economic developments such as the concentration of fishing on Dartmouth and Brixham.

Stokenham is already celebrated for the references to its fishing in a survey of 1309 (most recently published by H. P. R. Finberg in *West Country Historical Studies*, 1969). The manorial demesne included the ley at Slapton (a famous stretch of fresh water separated from the sea by but a bar of shingle) with its fishery (worth 10s. per annum). The customary tenants of the manor were expected to devote time to sea fishing on the lord's behalf as well as agriculture. Between February 2nd and the second Tuesday after Easter they were to station nine of their number, equipped with their own boats and tackle, by three rocks on the shore of the parish and there to take mullet. The mullet season coincides with that followed in these waters today. If the mullet was sold, the lord should have one third of the price or one third of the catch. The lord was also entitled to buy any porpoises caught (at 1s. a fish) and to give no more than a day's allowance of food for any salmon brought ashore. If the lord buys fish in the manor, he is to pay a penny for eight plaice, eight bream or one skate and to have a discount on the price of conger. In a later inquisition, the catching of ling is also mentioned.

That salmon continued to be caught on this shore is confirmed by their mention as an entry fine in the court rolls three hundred years later. That skate was also a common catch is seen in an entry for the 1579 court decreeing that no person 'garbage or bury any fish or wash any rays'.

The development of fishing settlements was a slow process. Initial building and village growth occurred away from the shore line unless the site was very sheltered. Men went to sea to fish but most will have had alternative sources of income on land. As there were no natural harbours in this parish, the boats being beached, there was no imperative that residence should be on the shore itself. Evidence of development in the later rather than earlier Middle Ages can be drawn from the Cornish villages of Looe, Mevagissey and Gorran Haven – all three examples of planned coastal development as the fishing industry gained importance and independent status. In Start Bay the normal pattern was for 'cellars' to be built on the shore, or to be developed out of caves. These were bases for the fisherman where tackle could be stored and fish processed. There are sixteenth century references to the 'capstander room', which one presumes to have housed machinery for hauling boats out of water. Cellars were properties that could be bought, sold or leased – frequently by people outside the village. Thus in 1632 William Gourney of Dartmouth had a fishhouse at Poke Hole, under the cliff at Hallsands.

The custumal of 1309 and later documents imply that the chief business of these fishermen was netting and long-lining rather than crabbing or shell fishing. Two forms of net were used, each based on shore. The first, a seine net, was launched to encircle shoals of mullet or mackerel, then hauled in by men on land. These shoals were spotted by men on cliff tops – in Cornwall they were called 'huers', in Stokenham 'hillmen'. This is doubtless the reason for the 1309 survey saying that the groups should be based on three rocks. There was even a little house south of Hallsands where the watchers could take shelter. This community also practised shore drag fishery. This was done with a tuck seine net of great length with a substantial bottom rope so that it dragged through the sea bed and disturbed the groundfish. Alarmed, they swam into the tuck at the end of the net – like a bunt, a great pocket. These nets needed to be long to get over the unproductive ground close to the beach. Thus, having anchored one end on land, a boat rowed by six men would pay out 1000 yards of net before returning over the same distance to a point two hundred yards downstream. Something of this size needed twelve men to haul it in.

Nonetheless, by the nineteenth century, crab, lobster and shellfish had become of prime economic importance. Netting was undertaken both to obtain a marketable catch, especially of mackerel and mullet, and for bait for the crab pots. The mullet season was at a time when crabbing was poor. Mullet could be stored for a day or two, giving time to alert the merchants, for example at Dartmouth. Not so mackerel which had to be removed as soon as it was caught. Were a shoal espied by the fishermen towards Start Point, a signal would be sent to Torcross whence would come the hawkers who distributed the catch amongst the villages and farms of the hinterland.

Crab bait needs to be a good firm fish such as were caught in the shore drag net or could be got from long-line fishing. To undertake the latter one needed bait as well. To this end, specially fine seines were used to catch sand eels. The crab bait also needs to be fresh. There is thus a tremendous cycle of work involved in maintaining a string of crab pots – netting, long-lining, baiting, shooting, lifting, re-baiting and so on. Much of this required intense group co-operation, of either family or occupational units. The intensity of communal life makes the destruction of such groups at Hallsands the more tragic.

The reciprocal relationship between fishermen and farmers in the parish is exemplified on the one hand by the custom of doing six weeks harvesting and, on the other, by the preservation in valleys and coombes of willow beds for the construction of crab and lobster pots – here in the South Hams invariably of the inkwell type. These beds have now mostly vanished, though there is one just behind the shore line at Beesands, the memory preserved only in names like Widecombe – valley of the withies. The pots too are but a memory, superseded by plastic and man-made materials. An article on this by Dorothy Wright, 'Lobster and Crab-pots in the South Hams' (*Transactions of the Devonshire Association, 1976*) reports the shortage of willow after the second world war as the withy beds were untended, demand slack and the area laid waste by the American landing exercises. Men began to make wire framed pots. These were improved by Browse Brothers of Paignton who began to mass produce them from 1963. Browse were also significant boat owners and shellfish processors. From 1968 a superior product has been patented by G. C. Nantes of Weymouth which is a plastic frame of the same profile as the osier pots. This has a plastic base lashed to the frame by strips of old tyre, a polypropylene netting over the whole and a fibreglass tube acting as an entry funnel – tied to the frame with a nylon rope. The bait is held in the centre of the pot by a rubber twist. Pots like this may last up to seven seasons. Being lighter, they are easier to handle and store on board ship. However, they will not cling to the sea bed in the way of an old pot, thus they may not be as efficient in single pot locations where the scour is strong. It is their greater ease of handling and lasting power that has contributed so much to the expansion of crab fishery in these waters in the last decade. Whereas an old boat with a crew of three might manage up to 100 pots, the new boats will have ten times that number and will be able to go further in search of new ground.

NOTE
The Elizabethan Court Rolls of Stokenham Manor 1560–1602, ed. W. A. Roberts, 1984
The Technology of the Traditional Start Bay Crab Fishery (Stokenham Occasional Papers, no. 5), Melvin Firestone, 1983

June

JUNE DIARY

There should be no whining about the weather. What better conditions could be imagined than the sunsoaked days of May and June? As there has been a little moisture as well, the garden grows visibly. So fast, indeed, that the plants we were looking forward to monitoring have sunk beneath a sea of goose grass and nettle. Feverish investment in old machinery may stay the advance of wilderness but is no substitute for time on hands and knees. The fox population is evidently burgeoning. We have suffered yet more losses. The ultimate insult is that Reynard waits until early morning before making his attacks. Once, he was spied by a neighbour who chased him off with his dog. On two other occasions, however, witnesses caught up with him only as he ate the prizes of his expedition. [1984]

One area that has seen much change in British restaurants during the last twenty years is that of buying in elements of the menu. It is less and less permissible to incorporate manufactured items. Nowadays, as a matter of course, one makes one's own bread, meringues, brandy snaps, biscuits of all sorts, jams, breadcrumbs, pickles and jellies. I am sure that this was not always the case. Fuelling the infrastructure of the menu is indeed the most expensive aspect of kitchen labour; perhaps one reason for its lapse in the '30s and '40s. That it is now expected by the customer is a measure of the development of the British palate. One dread Sunday when we had a lapse in the matter of meringues (rock hard and wrong), a lady was overheard hissing to her neighbour, 'They must have got them from the baker'. Even the baker would not have produced these. [1983]

Mr Rogers has begun to deliver courgettes. He has had conspicuous success with Cambridge Vigour strawberries under plastic. The first Cornish berries were not interesting, with an almost greasy texture (perhaps from a chemical treatment). Mr Rogers' were light on flavour until the weather improved. They are tart, but the balance is greater

with every day's sunshine. We have taken Cornish potatoes through Mr Rogers and they have not been bad though consistently large. His own pickings from his Maris Bards has proved much better: no bitterness, the skin rolls off with the thumb. Freshness is important with potatoes. It is, too, with asparagus. As they stale, so bitterness predominates. Mr and Mrs Lloyd's harvest at Dittisham got off to a slow start and has only now reached its zenith. Advice on cooking asparagus exposes many changes of fashion. Dr Kitchiner (1829) recommends bundles of 25 spears, well trimmed of their outside skin, to be cooked for twenty to thirty minutes but 'watch the exact time of their becoming tender'. Constance Spry (1956), cooking them vertically in boiling water, suggests 12 to 14 minutes. Colin Spencer, in *The Guardian*, writes that twenty minutes in the steamer may be necessary for larger spears and from five to eight minutes for the smaller. We have found the latter band about right for the best of the Dittisham produce. But then, their spears are not the Norfolk jumbos which do require longer. Mr Spencer is also correct in saying that careful timing is necessary to allow the full flavour of the vegetable to emerge. Raw, fresh asparagus, which is very nice cut in thin rounds has a taste like a nutty pea, not asparagus at all. [1983]

The Lloyds' asparagus was picked for the last time this week. It is being succeeded by their artichokes. It can tax one's ingenuity to think of things to do with the latter other than eat them as they are – an activity that is really not popular among our customers. A purée in a small tart case makes a nice trimming to roast meat; or the purée can be mixed with rice and wrapped in a lettuce leaf, sent out as an accompaniment to a loin of lamb. They are growing two varieties: Vert de Laon and Campania. [1982]

Artichokes have benefited from the better weather; the Verts de Laon are coming in large and plump without being coarse. Mr and Mrs Lloyd have also grown some excellent Italian breeds of spinach: Fabris, with a heart-shaped leaf, has been picked and Medina, with a lanceolate leaf, is to come. [1983]

Early crop raspberries are not best suited to our climate. The moisture is too great and the winters too warm. They suffer die-back. As the fruit is borne on last year's wood this reduces the crop. The Lloyds are planting mainly Malling varieties for the earlies. The autumn crop is better as they produce on this year's canes. [1984]

Adult guinea fowl – egg layers, not table birds.

Broad beans and spinach are two vegetables that have started coming in the last three weeks. One is constantly reminded of the need to get your broad beans off the plant before they become too big. Although some kind gardeners have brought microscopic pods (almost literal infanticide), none of them has been sweet enough to cook whole. We wondered if this was because of the slow growing conditions this year. Growers have been vexed with the very heavy rain combined with high winds. Some of our acquaintance have had their bean fields virtually flattened and their crops destroyed. [1981]

Mrs Griffin from Stoke Fleming, the lady that kindly supplies us with sea spinach, brought in rock samphire last week. It was turned into a sauce for turbot. Half a pound was cooked in a covered pan with six tablespoons of water for ten minutes, drained, blended with half a pound of melted butter and seasoned (not too much salt needed). Mrs Griffin says that they often eat gulls' eggs and blanched samphire, with a vinaigrette. [1982]

A visit was had from David Beazley, bearing peach leaves and a delicious ash key pickle. This was a sweet pickle of vinegar and sugar (as in Roger Phillips's *Wild Food*) and is to be recommended. The flavour of the keys themselves is light. We also heard of the summer truffle being used by Tim and Sue Cumming of the Hole in the Wall restaurant in Bath. It would appear that a lady of their acquaintance brings them in. She observes the antics of the squirrels beneath her beech trees towards the end of the summer. When they begin hyper-active scrabbling at one spot she makes a sortie with her fork and lo! truffles. Florence White talks of them coming from Batheaston and indeed it is in this parish that the squirrels have their home. By coincidence, Batheaston was the residence of C. E. Broome (1812–1886) a pioneer mycologist whose collections, in large part, are in the British Museum. The Cummings find that the flavour is not as intense as the French or Italian sorts and that they must be used very fresh. They put them in eggs *en cocotte* or in an omelette. [1984]

The last month has seen some very high fish prices and variable quality. It is not easy to maintain continuity when unsure of supplies or with materials that oscillate wildly in standard. Take, for instance, Dover soles: from one landing to the next, they have gone from fat to lean to fat again. Scallops, too, which we were given to understand were in eclipse for the time being, suddenly turn up in perfect condition. Lobster has been plentiful, but many of the fish have only recently shed their shells. They are therefore rather empty, the flesh is a little loose textured and the claw meat pappy. The taste is sweet, but not as good as when they have filled out their new carapace. It is not easy to judge a live lobster in this condition. The pundits say to squeeze it across the shoulders; if the shell gives, reject it. This is a sure way of doing it after they have been cooked but there is more resistance to a squeeze when alive. The most reliable way is to have a true judgement of weight for size so that you can tell if they are weighing light. [1983]

Lack of salmon in the early part of the season has been but one problem in the fish markets. Fears of overfishing have led to a blanket ban on landings of many flat fish, plaice, dabs and flounders from these waters. This caused many of the Brixham boats to go north-west and local markets proved most unsatisfactory. Some fish from Liverpool was seen down here, so poor was the home offering. The lack of flats may be the cause of more round, pelagic, varieties being brought in. Weavers were to be had – there was an outbreak of weaver poisoning on a south coast beach this spring (they bury themselves in the sand below high water mark and the hapless bather steps on the spine) – red bream and black bream too. The black bream Joyce Molyneux grilled with lemon and fennel in the gut and stuffed in slits down the sides (often the simplest way of dealing with round fish) and served a lemon and onion sauce (as in Colin Spencer). Sea bass have jostled with the humble mackerel for space under the grill; these latter served with an apple purée strengthened with some horseradish. Among the more exotic fish has been angel shark (rather muddlingly also called monkfish), rarely seen in Dartmouth. [1985]

There has been great mutability of cooking times over the years. In *The Caterer*, the chef of London's *Le Suquet* restaurant cooks a portion of salmon for three minutes in a cool oven. Later in the same issue, Michael Raffael reports the tendency to reduce the cooking of pork, now that parasites are less frequent and as caterers need to preserve moisture so as to maximise weights. Keith Thomas, in *Man and the Natural World* (1983) discusses earlier attitudes to blood: seventeenth century sects with scruples about blood in gravy and black puddings, but not about meat itself; Samuel Pepys's description of Mr Andrews who eats 'with no pleasure unless the blood run about his chops'. C. P.

Moritz and Per Kalm, eighteenth century visitors to England, both observed our taste for underdone meat. However, examination of a nineteenth century cookery book such as Dr Kitchiner shows that rare was not a concept encouraged by his instructions. Nevertheless, care was urged on the roaster of meat to keep the juices within the joint so that it should be succulent. Mrs Rundle counsels that salt be not put on the meat before roasting lest it draws the blood – a piece of advice that is often given today, though I fear we always salt our steaks before cooking. The good Dr Kitchiner suggests that careful managers will undercook a large joint so that it may be used on the morrow for a hash. But lamb, and all other young animals, should be thoroughly cooked 'till you see it drop white gravy'. Pork, of course, must be cooked through, for 'the sight of it is enough to appal the sharpest appetites, if its Gravy has the least Tint of redness'. The times given by Kitchiner indicate that beef, at least, was cooked medium to rare. He allows about fifteen minutes per pound for a 15lb joint before the fire. He also appreciates that people like their beefsteaks cooked in different ways: orders for underdone or thoroughly done steaks should be taken by the cook before the meal. Christopher Driver's *The British at Table* (1983) makes much entertaining use of the work of market research and related disciplines. One of his facts, from the Meat Promotion Executive, is that a taste for rare beef is limited to 10 per cent of the population. This proportion is confirmed by our experience at the Tall Ships, though not at the Carved Angel. [1983]

KID

In 1981 we cooked our first kid. It has since become a regular item on the menu. Not only does it have a flavour of value, but it is a meat that people are glad to encounter, so rarely can it be found in butchers' shops. Goat products have become more popular in England in the '80s. The fashion for allergies has given a boost to the consumption of goats' milk. Foreign travel has awakened esteem for goats' cheese and yoghurt. Goats are popular among smallholders and proponents of self-sufficiency; they take up marginal land and act as useful vegetarian scavengers when not eating people's prime seedlings and garden crops. With their increase has come a need to cull the billy kids from the herds. It is thence we draw our supplies. There is a small commercial traffic in kids, mainly between the larger goat keepers and the markets of the

Midlands where the Asian butchers will readily sell them. Our first kids were kept by a lady whose son was allergic to cow's milk. At first, we took them at a few days old. Later, we were accepting them at three or four weeks. Their dead weight, dressed, was about nine pounds. The bones are very large in proportion to the flesh and there is a gelatinous quality to the meat that makes it rich to eat although light in flavour.

They were cooked in two ways. The first was marinated, in joints, with lemon, oil and herbs then roasted for about twenty minutes in a hot oven. This was served with redcurrant jelly and bread sauce, making a gravy with the juices, white wine and stock. The second was to treat it as veal and make a *blanquette* with carrots and onions. Other dishes were added to the repertoire in later months. General opinion on sampling all of these is that the roast does it best justice. Kid does not have an extensive range in this country. E. S. Dallas, writing in *Kettner's Book of the Table* (1877), commented: 'There are stories of kid being sold for house-lamb. It is sad to think what the flesh of this little creature will grow to when it becomes a goat, or when old enough to be weaned. Too soon it turns to wickedness and folly. While it is still a suckling, however, it is very good, and may be roasted either as lamb or as hare clothed with bacon.'

Goat keeping in Dartmouth has a long history. There were 15 goats and 40 sheep on the demesne at Townstal in 1086. In the same survey (the *Exon Domesday*), the manor of Buckland had 26 goats to 56 sheep. This pattern is repeated throughout those regions whence we have livestock counts in the different versions of Domesday. In the eastern counties of Norfolk, Suffolk and Essex, there were 130,000 sheep, 31,000 pigs, 11,000 goats and 9,000 cattle and oxen. By the same token the cheese production of Somerset is shown founded not on cattle (used predominantly for tillage) but on sheep and goats. Chewton Mendip had 800 sheep and 50 goats; Stratton had 317 sheep and 43 goats; Pilton 500 and 42 and so on. That this population was not due to a propensity of the Norman invaders for goats' cheese is shown by a tenth century survey of the abbey lands of Thorney in Hatfield noting the presence of 47 goats alongside a flock of 250 sheep.

If goats had thus an honourable place in the farms of the Middle Ages, why did they fall out of favour? If we believe David Mackenzie's *Goat Husbandry* (1957), decline was due above all to the enclosure movement and the wayward habits of the goat. This, putting it at the eighteenth century, may be leaving it too late. Although Dr Thomas Muffet (1553–1604) mentions the consumption of goats in *Healths*

Improvement, counselling indeed that old goats should be baited, like bulls, to tenderise their flesh, an agricultural treatise of the same period, by Thomas Tusser, has no word for goats at all.

The tending of goats has certain drawbacks. They go feral at certain stages of their yearly cycle, requiring careful herding if they are not to break out. They are subject to parasites unless allowed free range. Their resistance to rain is low, thus needing permanent shelter. Their appetite is catholic and voracious. They are suited above all to small-scale subsistence farming, a tendency that English agriculture has been trying to rise above since the creation of the first sheep walks. Thus its disappearance from the fields of England may be quite early. Certainly, no goat is mentioned in the Tudor and Stuart court rolls of the manor of Stokenham, to name but one Devon village, and inventories for the county of the same period ignore them completely. Studies of Elizabethan trade with Morocco show us exporting, or re-exporting, saffron to North Africa, and returning with large numbers of goatskins (while at the same time being ourselves exporters of rabbit skins, calfskin and lambskin).

The animal may have disappeared more slowly in the highland zone. Both Wales and Scotland continued to keep and serve goat well into the eighteenth century. Mackenzie suggests the Highland Clearances as the mortal blow. Boswell and Johnson were served kid on their tour of the Highlands; Thomas Pennant (quoted by C. Anne Wilson, *Food and Drink in Britain*, 1973) notes in 1776 the popularity of kid in Wales as a winter meat. He also records the drying and salting of larger animals – 'splayed [i.e. spayed] goats of six or seven years' – called 'hung venison' and the same beasts being eaten fresh, called 'rock venison'. Mackenzie has a Highland recipe for smoking goat hams, using a 12 to 18 month castrate, sweet cured and then smoked for a fortnight over birch or juniper branches or oak sawdust. Eighty years later, George Borrow was to record a sight of goats feeding near Beddgelert in Caernarvon, 'beautiful creatures they were, white and black with long silky hair, and long upright horns. They were of large size, and very different in appearance from the common race. These were the first goats which I had seen in Wales; for Wales is not at present the land of goats, whatever it may have been'.

The revival of goat keeping dates from the Second World War. There had, of course, been a quickening of interest in the art in the late nineteenth century – the Goat Society was formed in 1879 – and the breed had been improved in subsequent years. Austerity created a new market for goat milk. Goats were not recognised as a productive animal, therefore their produce was not rationed. While cows' milk attained an ever wider distribution, anyone needing to supplement his allowance might need to turn to the goatherd. Feedstuff was subsidised, thus the goat keeper had cheap supplies and a market ready to pay over the odds. This shifted the centre of goat keeping from the poorer highlands (now in receipt of free cow's milk) to the Home Counties. Thence, the breed found a new springboard to launch its attack on the allergic and asthmatic town dweller and the self-sufficiency freaks of the bourgeoisie. As a result, the goat has never had it so good.

That said, there are still very few recipes specifically for goat although one might take to heart the advice of *Tante Marie* (1925 edition) that for all mutton recipes you may use lamb or kid. With more than a million head in France, it is surprising that the meat is not found more often on restaurant menus there. Enjoyment of the meat might be enhanced if steps were taken to improve its condition before slaughter. Castration at birth improves the rate of growth and meat–bone ratio. It is doubtful whether any goat-keepers consider the quality of meat on their male kids, they only seek to dispose of them as soon as possible.

I append some notes on recipes for kid to be found in cookery books. Elizabeth David (*Italian Food*, 1954 and *Mediterranean Food*, 1950) has notes, as you might expect from her subjects. A recipe for a *ragoût* with tomatoes and vegetables, white wine and Marsala and orange juice and coriander, and one for roast leg spiked with garlic and rosemary come from Italy; a shoulder stuffed with veal, pork, liver and spinach comes from Corsica.

The indefatigable Dr Kitchiner (*Cook's Oracle*, 1817) is one of the few older authors to include a note on roasting kid, 'A young sucking kid is very good eating', to be done in the manner of hare or fawn.

Morton Shand (*A Book of Food*, 1927) makes the comment, 'I expect we have many of us eaten goat at one time or another without being aware of the fact'; otherwise, he admits that kid can be palatable when roasted.

There is a recipe for roasting kid with garlic and rosemary, then making a sauce with the juices, flour and cider given by Bill Austin of Blostín's Restaurant in Shepton Mallet (*The Restaurant Recipe Book*, 1980). Cider apart, it is the E. David recipe from *Italian Food*.

Elisabeth Lambert Ortiz in her *Book of Latin American Cooking* (1984) includes a Peruvian recipe for a stew made with garlic, cayenne, coriander leaves, potatoes, peas and white wine. She also suggests a leg of kid dressed with mint and garlic as well as one dressed with a Venezuelan seasoning of olive oil, garlic and vinegar.

Jane Grigson's *Observer Guide to European Cookery* (1983) has a good recipe for kid from Portugal called *chanfana*. It is a strong red wine stew, the meat being marinated for twenty-four hours with sliced onion, cloves, bay leaf, parsley and quite a lot of paprika. It was originally intended for cooking in a baker's oven so the heat starts high and falls over a period of three hours (for a five pound piece of meat). The end result, tried with lamb this time, is a strong and spicy dish, the cloves and bay leaves contributing a lot to the taste. Except for the time involved, it is very easy.

Anne Willan includes a note about goats in her survey of French provincial cooking (*French Regional Cooking*, 1981). She observes that a *blanquette* is made in the Loire and Poitou after the springtime cull of male kids.

A modern French chef who does cook kid is Alain Chapel. His recipe for a stew with herbs, cream and small onions is in his *La cuisine est beaucoup plus que des recettes*. Jacques Médecin in *Cuisine Niçoise* (1983) has a massive stew of a whole kid with 20 red peppers, five and a half pounds of tomatoes, garlic and white wine.

As a region with a strong tradition of goat husbandry, Berry could be expected to produce at least one recipe. Printed in Renée Ledoux-Panis, *Le bon Manger et le bon Boire en Berry* (1981) is a gigot roasted with young garlic bulbs, pulled with the leaves.

The best collection is in Mackenzie's *Goat Husbandry* (1957). In early editions he included instructions for dealing with adult animals but these were scrapped 'as being a lost cause'. He has roast kid from central France, larded with garlic and bacon; leg marinaded with tansy, thyme, parsley and garlic, dill or caraway seeds, vinegar and oil, from the Alps. This is roasted slowly (Gas 2, thirty minutes a pound) with some of the marinade while a sauce is made with honey, vinegar and tomato purée. From Normandy comes kid cooked with spring onions and peas, similar to our duck with green peas. And, finally, from Sweden he has kid simmered in cream.

Stone Mill Goats

It was from the farm of Mr and Mrs John Pinnington at Stone, south west of Exeter, that we took some of our first kids. Their enterprise, now no longer, was an interesting example of adventurous marketing and hard work. At first, they kept mainly pigs, only building up the goats as they found them to be more profitable. They achieved a herd of about forty animals, kept for their milk, from which they made a variety of cheeses. The herd was made up of Anglo-Nubians, with lop ears and dark brown coats, and British whites.

Mrs Pinnington was the chief cheese maker. The farm had so large a market that it couldn't supply sufficient milk from its herd alone. Some milk, therefore, was bought from a neighbour. Distribution in England was handled by a wholesaler who markets health foods; more local marketing was undertaken by the Pinningtons themselves, their milk and their cheese relied upon by a substantial number of people incapable of digesting cows' milk.

Mrs Pinnington was emphatic that goats' milk need not taste radically different from cows'. The development of a goaty flavour is more often the sign of improperly milked and tended stock. It will taint if a billy is allowed to run with the herd. Further problems arise if the milk is not chilled rapidly after milking. Certainly the yoghurt we took from the farm tasted not at all of goats. The goat flavour develops in the making of cheese but, by then, this is desirable.

Mrs Pinnington made a feta cheese, a soft cream cheese, a hard cheese that keeps for a considerable time and a Coulommiers type. Latterly, she pasteurised her milk; she turned to this after problems with cultures.

While we have taken suckling kids for eating, the Pinningtons raised them to three months before slaughter. They were sure of their tenderness and flavour. When they have sold them to Greek restaurants, they have been appreciated, but the Greeks have missed the strength of flavour that comes from the scant pasture and the wild thyme and marjoram that constitute their Mediterranean diet.

GUINEA FOWL

'Guinea Fowls are only moderately interesting to eat, though they have their passionate admirers', observed Morton Shand (*The Book of Food*, 1927). Pomiane obviously thought the same (*Good Fare*, 1932): 'Guinea fowl is rarely served. It is a cultivated taste'. Dallas (*Kettner's Book of the Table*, 1877) was a little more enthusiastic: 'As the guinea fowl is in season from February to June, when game is scarce, it makes a good substitute. The eggs of this bird are very delicate.' The only recipe for eggs that I have found is in Wyvern's *Common Sense Cookery*

(1894) where he suggests them in aspic. Of course, in the poultry yard, guineas are feral creatures, flying about and laying eggs in the most unprepared spots in hedge and bank bottoms. To gather fresh eggs requires superhuman watchfulness. Crows, rats and weasels normally get there before you. Waverley Root was an old hand at guinea fowl. He reared them himself. The easiest way of bagging them, he thought, was shooting them where they perched. In *The Food of France* (1958) he noted this as the method employed in south western districts. Who can tell whether the game of their flesh was worth the candle of their desperate shrieking?

The guinea fowl, a bird distributed across much of Africa, was known to the Mediterranean world of ancient times. However, it dropped from view until its reintroduction through Portugal after the discovery of the Guinea Coast at the close of the fifteenth century. Well known, apparently, in Renaissance Europe, it went through a period of etymological flux as a turkey, or a *poulet d'inde* in France, before settling down to its own name to distinguish it from that other introduction, this time from the New World. Nonetheless, references in earlier cookbooks are sparse, not helped by this confusion of names. The Shorter Oxford gives the first use of the term guinea fowl to 1788 and of guinea hen to the late 16th century. In sixteenth and seventeenth century inventories of Devonshire and Oxfordshire, there are references to both turkeys and 'gennies' but it is uncertain to which species the first name applies. Neither is common; of 260 inventories from Devonshire, mainly seventeenth century, there are notes of two owners of 'gennies' and one of a turkey; from the same number of late sixteenth century inventories from Oxford, there appear two owners of turkeys, one a lady in St Ebbes, the other a wealthy yeoman of Witney who kept one cock and two hens in his inner courtyard. The eighteenth century seemed ignorant of its flavour; even Parson Woodforde, in poultry loving Norfolk, never consumed it. However, the household accounts of Viscount Courtenay at Powderham Castle south of Exeter in 1795 have a note that five guinea poults were bought in July. They cost 1s. 9d. as opposed to 9d. for a chicken. Matters improve with the nineteenth century. Dr Kitchiner suggests treating it like a pheasant; Eliza Acton recommends that you hang it as many days as the weather will allow; Mrs Rundle says too that you should treat it as pheasant, throwing in for good measure advice on its management: 'Guinea hens lay a great number of eggs; and if you can discover the nest, it is best to put them under common hens which are better nurses. They require great warmth; quiet; and careful feeding with rice swelled with milk or bread soaked in it. Put two peppercorns down their throat when first hatched'. (This last specific is meant to make them feel warm.) E. Duret (*The Premier Cookery Book*, n.d.) also thought the guinea a substitute pheasant, because its flesh was so dark.

This characteristic has changed in recent years. Now, it is a tastier alternative to chicken rather than a reminder of last winter's shoots. The plain fact is that although they used to taste like pheasant, they hardly do today; and if their flesh used to be dark, it is now a faint shade of coffee, no more. Waverley Root observed that some breeders had achieved a whiter fleshed bird and this was the sole genetic improvement yet known. (There is not the number of varieties found in chicken. You order chicks from a breeder and they come; different plumage colours bear no relation to eating or breed.)

References to the bird may be few in earlier literature, but it had a ready market in south Devon of the 1900s. Jessie Smaridge, remembering life in Buckland Tout Saints after the First World War, included this reference: 'I had gleanies [gliny, gleany: a Devon word for guinea fowl] too, always a brace of gleanies and they'd sell for seven and six a brace. I was making a fortune, but how much are they now? Mr Shirell or Shirwell came from Teignmouth but Mr Hayes always came to us. They were butter dealers and when they came down, if there was a chance of anything from the gun or traps he would take that from us.'

Guinea fowl are largely available as frozen birds, mass produced in Norfolk and elsewhere. Dartmouth is blessed, however, with a small grower, Mr A. B. Brook of Millcombe, Blackawton. He came to them out of curiosity, wanting to produce something for which there was a perceived demand yet was not subject to competition from large-scale enterprise. He buys day-old chicks from a specialist in Aberdeen; he rears them until they are ten or twelve weeks and then begins to kill. At first he thought that demand would be stable throughout the year, but he had reckoned without south western seasonality. He will produce until the end of the summer then gradually wind down until left with no birds by Christmas. He kills by wringing their neck. Henry Smith (*The Master Book of Poultry and Game*, n.d., *c*.1950) reckons this important so that no blood is lost, the meat having a tendency to dryness. They must be plucked almost at once. He dips in hot water and puts them on the plucking machine. The feathers are hard stuck so only 95 per cent come off in the machine. Hand finishing can be done at the rate of a dozen an hour. They are drawn and trussed, to be sold oven ready.

Guineas look much larger in their copious plumage. A three month bird will not weigh more than three pounds with the gut in. They will grow larger, but old birds are not recommended – again because of toughness and dryness.

Summer production may run at a hundred a fortnight. Any that are not sold fresh, for the killing is predetermined, have to be frozen, for sale through local butchers. The birds live indoors all the while (reduces the noise factor) on litter, in batches of about a hundred. They have room to exercise their wings and will roost on the rafters. When they first arrive, they are fed BOCM starter compound but they are soon moved on to a home-made meal of wheat, soya, barley and fish meal. They have added mineral salts and vitamins, but no antibiotics or growth promoters. The fish meal is necessary to give adequate protein content but is reduced as they get older to avoid tainting the flesh. Home production of the meal is not only more economical, for Mr Brook is a farmer as well, but enables him to vary its content according to progress.

The difficulty in plucking means that they are hung nude, unlike game. Most guineas are not hung at all but we have experimented, as has Mr Brook, with this treatment. We have had them swathed in a plastic bag, to preserve moistness not modesty, and hung them for four (warm) days to a week. Mr Brook feels there is little improvement by hanging; we thought there was, and that there was no desiccation.

The putative latter-day decline in flavour may have more to do with rearing and breeding than treatment *post mortem*. Perhaps more free range combined with a final fattening period would do the trick. Alexandre Dumas observed in his encyclopaedia that 'when the guinea hen is raised at liberty in a park, its flesh is equal in delicacy to a pheasant'.

I find it hard to understand why the books talks of guineas being in season from February to June, although it may have to do with breeding cycles. We no longer think in these terms for domestic fowl but I was taken by references to seasonality of hens' egg production in Marshall's *Rural Economy of the West of England* (1796).

The only circumstance that struck me, in Devonshire, with respect to this petty article of livestock, was the scarcity of eggs compared with the numbers of fowls. The markets of Plymouth, I understand, are supplied with eggs, in some considerable part, from the north of Devonshire; from whence they are sent, twenty or thirty miles, by land;

and this while, to common appearance, there are a sufficient number of fowls kept, within ten miles of it, to supply all its wants of this article.

This circumstance did not strike me, until I had spent some time in Scotland; where, from no greater appearance of fowls, the quantity of eggs consumed in the country, and the extraordinary quantity sent, especially from Berwick, to the London market, is almost incredible.

These extraordinary facts led me to a closer investigation of this subject, than I had, theretofore, thought it entitled to; and it evidently appears that the whole disparity of produce may be traced to a disparity of management.

In Scotland, fowls in general roost in the warm smokey cottages of their owners; are nurtured, and forced in a hot house. The consequence is, they produce eggs in every season; and, generally speaking, the year round. The gentlemen of Scotland, seeing the superiority of the cottage fowls, in their productiveness of eggs, have removed the comparative sterility of their own, by keeping them, literally, in hot houses; *– built on a similar principle to those in which exotic plants are conserved; flues being formed in the walls; with niches or small recesses, on the inside, for the fowls to lay and breed in; with roosts for them to rest on at night.*

The same sort of fecundity is well known to be produced, by the warm livery stables of London.

On the contrary, in Devonshire, fowls roost in the cool open air; frequently in trees; in a state of nature.

The fowl, in its native woods, probably bred only once a year; and, of course, produced eggs at no other season; and, I think, we may fairly infer, that the nearer they are suffered to approach that state, the less fruitful they will prove.

July

At times like these, who needs the Mediterranean? Dartmouth basks in sunshine, a tingling breeze off the sea brings the night stillness to bearable cool; yachts, ferries, ships, submarines and dinghies chunter around the harbour from dawn to dusk (not everyday visitors, the submarines); long queues form for the pleasure boats. Occasionally you are brought up short by a pile of chip papers and ice cream cones in a dusty corner, but the streets are bedecked with flowers – for Britain in Bloom – and all is well with the world. [1983]

The growth of salad stuff and herbs in our own garden has accelerated in recent days. We are able, on a good day, to offer infant specimens of two sorts of cut-and-come-again lettuce, one American and one Italian, some brown edged Italian lettuce, purslane, salad burnet, comfrey, chop-suey greens and wild chicory. Unfortunately the red chicory has not germinated. [1981]

Our qualified success with burnet and rocket has not been repeated this year. We bought some rocket plants but they turned out to be flowers rather than edible leaves. The burnet failed to germinate, as too did the dill. Additions to salads have been confined to shredded sorrel, dandelion, pot marigold and borage flowers. [1982]

David Beazley, Joyce's right hand in the kitchen, has taken to seeking out chanterelles. He has had some success. He points out that the season for their capture is from July to September and that the two hunting grounds he has so far found have had in common beech trees, sandy soil, moss and moisture. [1982]

Another fungus gathered by David Beazley was Chicken in the Wood, from Holne Chase near Ashburton. This is full of texture and delicious in taste, raw or cooked. Roger Phillips (*Wild Food*, 1983) states that it is popular in the USA, perhaps we should value it as well. High season for

Izabella Carroll in front of the maturing racks of Sharpham cheese.

gatherers may be the autumn, but there is much to occupy them now, if assiduous. The elderflowers have done their duty, from fritters to jam; wild strawberries, smaller than any you have seen, for tiny tarts, came from David Beazley; blueberries in large quantity from the same source, as well as wild cherries. Samphire is finished for the time being, though there may be a second growth of young leaves after flowering. [1984]

This is the best time of year for potatoes and, generally, we have been lucky with our supplies. Our one mischance was taking some Cornish that had been hanging around the shop for too long. Their age caused bitterness. This recalled a comment by a gastronomic jury in Jersey that, although a centre for early potatoes, many of the restaurants were serving bitter tubers. Is it freshness, storage or variety? Admiral Haynes is indefatigable in his garden and has grown five varieties this year. We tried them the other night and our collective thoughts, in order of preference, were:

Suttons Foremost – very waxy (the Admiral, who likes a floury potato, called them soapy), white colour, tasted the most like new potatoes (a built-in memory common to all of us, like fresh bread).

Sharps Express – a larger tuber that took the longest to cook, but a firm flesh and sweet taste.

Arran Pilot – slightly floury, but fair taste.

Home Guard – floury, nonetheless decent taste. They were difficult to scrape. This is the standard Cornish variety available in Devon shops.

Ulster Sceptre – came off badly by comparison with the others, especially as it is now the commonest commercial variety here. We have not found it so bad as on this occasion. These were difficult to scrape, slightly bitter in taste and too floury, almost wet. Yet they were not overcooked and they had all been dug at the same time.

We have also had *Maris Bard* from Mr Rogers, quite a firm potato, very white, with mild flavour; and *Pentland Javelin* from Capton – this has proved a good variety. [1983]

We have observed an improvement in the varieties of redcurrant produced commercially: larger fruit, with a more generous taste. Private growers with perhaps long established bushes of indeterminate variety often provide small fruits, more skin than flesh and very difficult to take off the stalk. We have been having a mild glut of these, causing us to look to our recipes for redcurrant jelly. Joyce Molyneux emphasises the worth of Eliza Acton's original, rendered by Elizabeth David and Jane Grigson: equal weight of currants and sugar, boiled together for eight minutes, stirring and skimming all the while, then sieved to take off a jelly of great clarity and luminescence. Miss Acton observed, even then, that the Norman currants were of 'richer quality' than our own and that the Normans, from whom this recipe emanated, needed to boil their fruit for one, not eight, minutes. (Mrs David says *two* minutes; her edition of Eliza Acton may be different from mine.) It has also been good to see white currants, from Mrs Harvey in Slapton, only an occasional delivery having been made hitherto. They are much smaller than their red and black cousins, doubtless because their strains have not been improved. [1982]

Fish has been in fair supply, prices holding firm but quality good. Dover soles have started to come in more profusion although lemons are on the decline. Other flat fish, such as Torbay soles and dabs, difficult to find a month ago, are now plentiful. The salmon had a good month in May/June but have become less reliable in recent weeks. We have again had pale coloured fish. Lobsters have been uncommonly common. We have never been offered so many. I am not sure whether this is due to the fishermen's problems of selling them in the larger markets or reflects the position on the sea bed. Crabs have remained a problem: many small but few large; scallops have been very good. It was interesting last week to inspect Mr J. Distin's boat after a morning's fishing with a few inshore pots and a net strung out by the river mouth to catch bait. His pots yielded one or two lobsters and a dozen small crabs, mostly hens. Hens command half the price of cocks. Mr Glassbrook the fishmonger will not buy them because their smaller ratio of claw to body meat makes their picking uneconomic and because he finds the flavour inferior. Mr Distin had a good bucket of velvet crabs and three good-sized spiders. Hermits he had none. The net he put out had a varied catch including a large grey mullet which poached better than I had expected. Usually the fish is muddy in flavour. They are bottom feeders and many of the specimens brought into us are caught by river netsmen or fishermen, often as a by-product of salmon netting. Mr Distin was still working in the sea and the flesh had a cleaner taste. He also had some wrasse of marvellous size and colour – normally exported to the West Indian communities in the Midlands – and dog fish, sometimes sold as rock salmon, with a pinkish, firmish flesh. The wrasse I use for fish soup, the dog fish I tried for the first time – of moderate flavour. [1982]

Lamb from Luscombe in Totnes has been of very good quality this month. Otherwise there has been little of novelty or interest, except an Open University lecture listened to by Joyce Molyneux on the beef and meat trades. It was stressed that what was needed for the consumer was meat of red colour with minimal fat – the contrary to our own requirements. What is always strange about such discussions is that no thought of eating comes into them. It is as if the meat trade's responsibilities end with the sale of the meat not its consumption. [1982]

LANGAGE FARM, PLYMPTON

Langage Farm's arrival in Dartmouth with Jersey cream was a signal breakthrough in the search for satisfactory base materials. We had had farm cream before, but its manufacture was uneven and delivery hazy.

Home production began in 1980. Here was a herd of 250 milking Jerseys, supported by a further 150 heifers, hangers-on and two bulls, divided between two farms of 270 acres in aggregate. The price paid to the producer by the Milk Marketing Board (oh! what a whipping boy) did not fully reflect the high butterfat that had been achieved through careful breeding. The price was graded according to richness, but the MMB's maximum was below that of Langage. With all this work going apparently to waste, and the happy availability of Peter Tremain to combine with the owners Mr and Mrs Harvey in organising the venture, it was decided to go it alone. From a base range of clotted cream and double, single and whipping, the dairy can now offer its own creams, plain and flavoured yoghurts, cream and cottage cheeses (again plain and flavoured) and ice creams. It also sells butter (made by the local Co-operative Society) and hard cheeses, so that its range should be comparable to St Ivel and Eden Vale (Unigate and Express Dairy respectively).

The ideal for any dairy is that the whole production of the herd should be used for commercial sale. There is obviously a vast output of skimmed milk after cream separation. This can be fed to livestock. The MMB indeed pays 30p a gallon on skim fed to pigs (although it must be pasteurised for sale to outsiders). Without this, the initial economy of the dairy might have been more tenuous than it proved to be. However, there is now a real prospect of its discontinuance, which has caused Langage to think harder of ways to consume the skim in commercially useful lines. The burgeoning of yoghurt sales has helped (perhaps the fastest growing thing at present); so, too, the soft cheeses. Ice cream is seen as very important. New machinery is being installed to make their own, for sale through a farm shop, to the large population of Plymouth on their doorstep. This commercial development can be viewed as entirely the result of shifts in subsidy payments, not a response to taste or mass gastronomy. Had there not been a real possibility of the discontinuance of the skim milk subsidy, no effort would have been made to exploit the market for 'real' ice cream.

Daily milk production is of the order of 2,000 litres. There are two milkings, at five o'clock, morning and evening. Although yields will go up and down according to the season and the weather, there will not be a great variation week by week. The cows are kept indoors throughout the winter; to protect the ground as much as the beasts. A third daily milking has been known, but is uncommon. Constant production should be matched by constant consumption but this is far more difficult to engineer. The local economy is seasonal; cream is needed more during the summer months for fruits etc. and many of the farm's customers close down in the winter, for instance pick-your-owns. This is a further argument for ice-cream making. They have also installed a blast freezer of giant capacity both for ice creams and for freezing clotted cream. The ideal customer is a restaurant or hotel with a good year-round trade. To cope with peaks and troughs, the farm deals daily with the MMB. If there is insufficient demand for cream, then some of the milk from the farm will be sold to the Board; if on the other hand they need more milk, then a tanker can deliver from another farm with Channel Island cattle. It is possible, at the busiest time of the year, that up to 50 per cent of the milk is bought in. This is for a few weeks only.

Clotted cream takes up to 50 per cent of the produce of the dairy. This is Devon. It is made on three mornings of the week; the other things – yoghurts and cheese – being done in the aftermath. Milk stored in tanks from the parlour must be separated, pasteurised and tested for butterfat content before being cartoned and then cooked to make the clotted cream. Channel Island milk has a naturally high butterfat content, 5.3 per cent as opposed to the 3.7 per cent of a Friesian herd. Furthermore, the globules of butterfat are larger and thus more difficult to fix satisfactorily. Dairymen would recommend a mix of 90 per cent

Friesian and 10 per cent CI for a simple raw material. If the fat globule is not fixed, for instance through separating when the milk is at too low a temperature, there will be a greasy coating to the mouth. This, more than anything, seems to be the problem of mass-produced creams. Pasteurisation was not employed at Langage when they started in business. No doubt that raw cream will have greater opportunity of developing interesting flavours but using raw milk had very great drawbacks. In the first instance there was product variation and a less stable shelf-life (the customer is a hard taskmaster, especially when an anonymous purchaser in a health-food store); in the second, the attentions of the Environmental Health Department can become intrusive (understandable); in the third, unpasteurised skim milk cannot be sold to outsiders for pigs (a necessity in the early days before a balanced internal economy was created).

Just as pasteurisation removes some of the beneficent organisms from the milk, so too does machine separation. The natural process of separation is to let the milk from two milkings stand until the cream has risen; rising, therefore, on a liquid stuffed full of bacilli giving out interesting tastes. Separation cuts short this maturation. The author Cecil Torr, whose *Small Talk at Wreyland* (3v. 1918–23) is a classic of Devon literature, decried changes in south Devon in the second half of the nineteenth century.

Writing to my father (on 8 March 1846) my grandfather says: 'I do not think many of the agriculturalists are prepared for the very great changes that the railways will make.' But those great changes never came, as the agriculturalists never grasped the situation. So long as transport was difficult, each district had to grow nearly everything that it required. When transport was made easy, each district should have grown what it grew best. Here in the South Hams there was quite the best cream in England, and about the best cider, and also excellent mutton. Had people kept to things like these, and laid down all their arable land to grass, they would have saved far more on agricultural buildings, implements and horses, than they would have spent in getting arable products from a distance. And they would hardly have felt the depression that began in 1878, as that scarcely touched these things.

Being short sighted, they neglected their orchards, and grew careless of their cider-making, till Devonshire cider was out-classed by Hereford. And now they are ruining the cream by using separators. Of course it is cream made in Devonshire, but it is not what was known as

Devonshire cream. The stuff is not worth eating; but I suppose people will go on eating it as Devonshire cream, just as they go on drinking the wines of well-known growers, whose vineyards were exhausted years ago.

If you were making clotted cream, separation and rising would be fixed by heating on the top or the side of the stove. The cooked cream could then be lifted off the skim. I asked a friend who had a house-cow on her farm on Dartmoor for more information about making clotted cream at home, our own efforts being continually foiled by the local Guernsey's milk being below par, being needed for the calves, etc. She would reckon to make the cream by the Cornish rather than the Devon method. In other words, she lets the milk stand for a day (the colder it was, the better the rise) before skimming the cream off. The Devon method is to clot the cream while still on the milk. You are then left with cooked milk which no one, save pigs, likes unless you are prepared for a succession of milk puddings.

The cream that you have lifted off the top of the raw milk is placed in a vessel, for instance an enamelled setting-pan, which in turn goes into a water bath. Heat the milk by this indirect method to 80°C / 180°F and then cool it. The advantage of the Cornish method is that, having dispensed with pints of skim milk beneath the cream, the bowl can be smaller and more manageable. A disadvantage is lower productivity; skimming raw cream is more difficult than cooked. My informant also found that it was easier to make butter from clotted cream than from raw milk. It avoided that slight rancidity that often comes with home-made butter.

Making your own clotted cream is both easier and more difficult than it might appear. Easier, because the temperature is not as important as all that, provided you do manage to heat it up gently over a long period. If you fail to achieve 80°C / 180°F you will still get a lovely cream with excellent flavour, but you will lack the hard crust; more difficult, because managing the quantities of milk needed to produce a useful amount of cream can be messy and chaotic. You do need a double boiling arrangement, otherwise you are bound to overheat and that way lies disaster. For the first few times you may be content to heat the cream gently, even on the side of the kitchen range, so as to obtain no more than a set, rather than a crusty clotted. It is still delicious, as is *crème fraîche*, with innumerable flavours to it from the workings of the microbes.

At Langage, the milk is separated and pasteurised, tested for butterfat content, adjusted, and then potted up for cooking in ovens. The pots in which it is cooked are those in which it is sold. The cream is held at 90°C / 194°F for about half an hour. It is then capped or heat-sealed. In large production units, the cream is cooked then potted while still sufficiently liquid to undergo this process. Thus, it is never truly clotted. The whole cycle from separation to cooling for the large trays of clotted takes perhaps 48 hours although the smaller quarter-pound pots can be put through in a day.

Clotted cream will have a butterfat content in excess of 55 per cent. Double (48 per cent), whipping (35 per cent) and single (18 per cent) are the products of the separator and are stored in refrigerated milk tanks with agitators. It is interesting to compare the performance of Langage whipping against the big dairies' double. Many customers will happily use the lower grade of CI cream in preference to the top grade of mass-production.

As already mentioned, yoghurt sales are on the increase. Recently, the mode of production has been improved to the benefit of taste and texture. Yoghurt consists of skimmed milk, an addition of dry milk powder (separated milk solids) and perhaps of cream, if the butterfat content is incorrect. The Langage product is low fat. The culture used is fresh each time, not from the last batch as a starter. When they began, they used to use a starch to thicken. However this has been discarded as they improved their recipe – using steam rather than water to heat the cooking vessel, holding it at a higher temperature for longer. The end result is a plain yoghurt that stands comparison, in our eyes, with any available today.

Embarking on a programme of retail sales is no small jump for a farmer attuned to the demands of marketing and production Boards. Capital costs run high if a scale commensurate with the farm's own production is to be reached. Over £16,000 worth of packaging may be held at any one time. Machinery to deal with milk has to be well made and well maintained. It is thus expensive. One might think of capital to the tune of £100,000. Then there are the rounds, the sales force and the vehicles. One may finance much out of revenue (growth in cream sales is at 20 per cent per annum), but the profit margins are not high and competition from the big dairies is fierce. There was a noticeable change in policy on the part of Unigate to consumers such as the Carved Angel when Langage began to make inroads on the market. Now, Unigate is trying to play down the image of mega-business. Cream marketed in

Devon is to go out under the name of Daw's Dairy. This I find comparable to the playing with image that the large supermarkets indulge in; fooling us that we are buying something small and hand-crafted. This trend is at its worst in the in-store bakeries where we find the bread as bad, if not worse, than many big bakery products.

CRAB AND LOBSTER FISHING

Over the river from Dartmouth is that mass of land with Kingswear on the one side and Brixham on the other. Between the two towns is a stretch of rocky coast, culminating in Berry Head, site of many of the travails and dramas of the small lobster and crab boats of the Dart.

Kingswear parish almost qualifies for the French description of *presqu'île*. It is linked to the mainland by an isthmus that can have once been no more than a mile wide. The headland is split by deep valleys leading to Noss on the west, Man Sands and Scabbacombe on the east. The higher ground is open and bracing. In common with many coastal villages, original settlement was inland: Kingston in Kingswear as Townstal in Dartmouth or Upper Brixham in Brixham. Sensible people did not take to the water's edge until they had the technology and economic incentives to depend on marine activities. Dartmouth only got its church in the fourteenth century (not granted full parochial status until much later); Kingswear was not settled until the twelfth century; Lower Brixham, by the harbour, did not have a parish church until 1826 (the first incumbent was H. F. Lyte, author of 'Abide with me').

Also common to many villages in the district, settlement was scattered in small hamlets. Certainly these hamlets, bartons or isolated farms add to the enjoyment of wandering on foot: Brownstone, Coleton, Kingston, Nethway, Bookhay, Woodhuish and Raddicombe. In more recent times, a few have been elevated to the status of country houses with dependent cottages: Nethway, a foursquare seventeenth century mansion; Lupton, early nineteenth century; Churston, eighteenth century; and Coleton Fishacre, the most recent of them all, built for a D'Oyly Carte. They stamp the fields with a veneer of gentry and minor aristocracy. During the last century, the coast and river mouth at Kingswear has seen the building of large villas protected by pine woods from promiscuous entry but, for more gracious riverine architecture, the tourist should go upstream: Sharpham by Sir Robert Taylor, Sandridge by John Nash, Greenway opposite Dittisham put the late nineteenth century dwellings in Kingswear to shame.

The administration of the port of Brixham was for long the care of officials resident in Dartmouth, who supervised customs matters and the registration of boats for the coast from Torbay to beyond Salcombe. This reflected the medieval importance of the town. But although lumped together in this way, each harbour had a very different pattern of development. Dartmouth, the earliest centre, plumped for international trade, ultimately revolving around the exploitation of the Newfoundland connection. Salcombe, slower in taking off, served as an export centre for the grainlands behind Kingsbridge and as a base for a large fleet of schooners that tramped worldwide and had a speciality in fruit imports from the Atlantic seaboard. Brixham had a general trading base, servicing the growth of the Torbay district, but concentrated on fishing. The result was the largest fleet in the county – the source of British trawling skills. Its intrepid fishermen were the first to explore the riches of the North Sea banks – giving rise to the east coast ports as well as to a nomadic existence of six months away in either the North Sea or the Bristol Channel. The pre-eminence of Brixham faltered with the town's refusal to adopt steam power. A. M. Northway, in a study of boat ownership, identifies in this region a healthy self-reliance and independence – a long tradition of owner-operation – unlike the east coast fleets of Hewitt and Morgan; this, perhaps, the reason for the strength of liberalism and nonconformity in Brixham. Dartmouth, by contrast, was controlled by fleet-owning merchants and, save for a nineteenth century lurch towards Reform, has been more high church and more conservative.

Dartmouth was never a major English fishing port. In the census of 1841 there were recorded 94 mariners and sailors against 8 fishermen. (The record is not conclusive for there were also 150 people away on sea voyages, some of whom may have been fishermen.) Its interests lay in trade or the Newfoundland fisheries. As those activities declined, the town continued to see its salvation in the oceanic seaways, this time as a coaling station, a naval, or even a passenger, harbour. Fishing was the profession of a handful of small boat owners. Even if Defoe witnessed the onrush of a shoal in the river and was able to buy lobsters on the quay, Chaucer's shipman was the paradigm.

This has changed in the years since 1945. The town's maritime ambitions vanished with the shifts of world shipping and the disappearance of the steam vessel. However, successive governments have legislated to preserve and encourage inshore fishing and have protected some of the earning capacity of the fishermen through social security regulations. The Cod War and the rising cost of fuel have reinforced these measures. Technical improvements in crab and lobster gear have made the pursuit of these prey economically viable. Co-operative arrangements for marketing have enhanced the productivity of the boats. While Brixham witnessed a revival of the small trawler, Dartmouth and Kingswear concentrated on shellfish. Kingswear quay, from the early seventies, was the most important crab port in the UK. In 1970–75, 68 per cent of the English crab catch came from the south coast, as opposed to 31 per cent from the east and a minute quantity from the west. This was a complete reversal of the position that obtained in 1934–43 when 89 per cent of the catch was landed in east coast ports and 9 per cent in the south. In 1983, the south Devon contribution to the nation's crabmeat consumption was in the region of 33 per cent. The annual value of shellfish landings in Devon was £2.5 million. The top four ports in 1975 were Kingswear, Salcombe, Plymouth and Weymouth. Experts will have it that the shift does not represent a decline in crab stocks on the eastern littoral, rather a change in the pattern of fishing as men from those towns took up more trawling. The rise of the south west has coincided with the explosion of capacity with the adoption of plastic and nylon pots and the development of Decca Navigator equipment that can locate strings of pots in open seas with absolute facility. Thus not only has crabbing increased as an occupation but each boat has been able to catch more. Little wonder, then, that the English catch rose from 55,000 cwt in 1967 to 112,000 cwt in 1976.

The shellfish fleet in Dartmouth and Kingswear can be divided into two: those boats that fish in deep waters, mid-Channel and those that remain inshore. The former, with a crew of three, have a cabin and wheelhouse and can support a trip of up to 18 hours. They will still go out and in again in a day, unless they choose to land in a port away from home, for example Alderney or Cherbourg. The smaller craft, occasionally with a single operator, more usually with a crew of two, will stay in sight of shore. They may have a wheelhouse but they are open boats with few comforts. There were 26 boats operating out of Dartmouth in 1983, with a crew of 62. Of these, about a dozen are small inshore operators. Many of the larger boats are owned by shore-based proprietors, with the crew taking shares. The small craft are owner operated. One of these owners, Robert Dart, supplies us with many of the lobsters served at the Carved Angel. He fishes alone, going out in most weathers to pots disposed along the Kingswear to Brixham shore.

About nine other boats work this stretch. Robert has 140 pots distributed over three miles of shore line, some with a view to catching crabs, others lobsters. Both species inhabit rocky ground, lurking in fissures and nooks awaiting carrion. In palmier days, a man could earn a living from his knowledge of the tide-line, luring and hooking lobsters out of their crevices. Woe betide him if his exploring hand encountered a crab; their grip is as a vice, the choice might be to sever the finger or die by drowning on the incoming tide if the crab could not be dislodged from his lair. Whereas the crab is an active beast, responding well to the encouragement of fresh bait in pots, and wandering around the sea bed in search of food, as well as moving according to the ebbs and flows of tidal drift, the lobster is idle. It also loves, as does the prawn, the rotten and putrid that the crab would eschew. Robert Dart has nicked the tails of undersized lobsters before returning them to the sea. The following season he has found them again, in the same spot.

A sandy ground will yield a harvest, but mainly of she-crabs. They go there in the winter, as part of large scale movements connected with spawning. Typically, it is the female that does the work, cock crabs that have been tagged are found to indulge in little or no travel. Leaving pots on sandy ground is dangerous for there the trawlers operate and the likelihood of fouling the trawl is high.

On a week in the summer of 1983, Robert had five strings laid down. Three were laid off-shore across three submerged rocks and two were close to the Kingswear coast. Knowledge of the nature of the ground fifty feet under water is a skill that causes wonder. The mental map of the sea bed must be precise, yet it existed long before skin divers and television cameras brought us images to make concrete our speculations. The placing of the strings across the rocks far beneath the gunwhales of the boat has to be exact to avoid the outer pots being scooped up by a trawler. Robert Dart does not have any technological assistance from radio beacons and the like; he does it by eye, lining up features on the shore. So one string is dropped by taking a line through the Black Rock to the Day Beacon; the second by setting a cave in Ivy Cove with a hedge on the cliff above; the third by lining up a double hedge above Scabbacombe Head. Between the Bull, the name of one of these submerged rocks, and the shore there is a large rectangle of rocky ground that is good for cock crabs. You reach it by sailing out on a line from Scabbacombe until you can see Torquay round the headland. If your skills are developed to a high enough pitch, some of these things can be done in the fog. Robert is well able to guide errant yachts towards the mouth of the river when their navigators have no idea where they might be.

If some of the skill of crabbing and lobster fishing is knowing where to place your lure, the hard work is in its lifting, baiting and setting again. The pace of the task is set by the capstan. The line attached, it hauls in the string, giving you, just, time to remove the catch, set the bait and drop over the side before the next pot appears. Accidents, as cold hands get enmeshed in hawsers and grinding machinery, are frequent. Strings need to be attended to regularly if their catches are not to escape or die. Robert will lift his inshore strings each day, weather permitting, but those further out to sea may be left for alternate days, except in the autumn when catches are heavy. Managing this flock of pots has many parallels with the life of a goatherd or shepherd on dry land – the added ingredient being the cunning of the hunter. It is a full time occupation for a man and enough to keep a family. It pays better on the bigger boats, where the catches are heavier but the life is less natural: daily departures at two or three in the morning, a forty mile motor to the grounds, preparing the bait on the open deck, a hard grind hauling strings of a hundred pots or more in very heavy weather before homecoming in the mid-afternoon.

It is a common complaint that things used to be different, but there is a serious problem from over-fishing. The large craft avoid it by going further afield, but the inshore operator needs to be concerned. Exploitation of the ground has been so intense in recent years that fishery scientists have voiced doubts of its continuance without precautionary measures. There were 46,000 cwt of crabs landed at Devon ports in 1975; by 1982 this has reduced to 39,000 cwt. The minimum size for lobsters and crabs has been raised in an effort to preserve stocks but it may be that decades of rest will be needed to rebuild populations. Robert's harvest, one morning in June, was seven lobsters, seven cock crabs and two-thirds of a chest of she-crabs; by no means a princely income and subject to the whims of weather, prey and market.

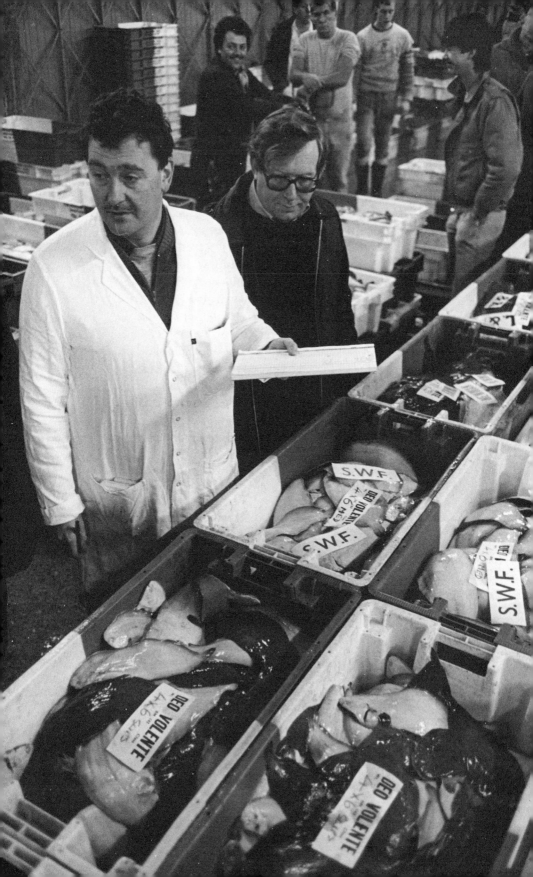

August

David Beazley's propensity for gathering has yielded good dividends. First he went up-river for wild cherries – very small and sharp – which we have macerated in brandy. Next he returned with a large box full of chanterelles, evidently enjoying the rain that has recommenced, some earth balls and rowanberries. [1982]

Samphire has continued to adorn our plates and we had a present from Dr and Mrs George Tee of a jar of their own samphire, pickled to John Evelyn's specification. Though a strong pickle, the taste of the plant still came through. We have done our own using half cider and half vinegar. Joyce Molyneux has also put some cuttings into her allotment, hoping that they will root. Cassell's *Dictionary of Cookery* observes that they may 'sometimes successfully [be] cultivated in beds of sand, rich earth and rubbish occasionally sprinkled with a little salt.' [1982]

Thanks to M. F. K. Fisher's books being republished in paperback, we were moved to try a first course of steamed vegetables with accompaniments. Although reasonable at home, it has always seemed a dangerous offering for a restaurant. It is difficult to get the timing right, cooking more than one vegetable at once (we did courgettes, carrots, peas, mange-touts, beans, calabrese, tomatoes and green peppers – or at least five of these at once). And the seasoning is not so easy either. Everyone says that the natural salts are preserved in the steaming process so that less seasoning need be added, but something still had to be done. Try as we might, we had difficulty getting the vegetables to absorb the aroma of any herbs that we might put in the steaming water. This is perhaps simpler with something that retains moisture, for instance fish. All this showed that dreams at bedtime do not necessarily work in a hard-pressed kitchen. Affairs that seem effortless in French three-star houses or on the pages of a book need a lot of effort before they are right for you.

To make the vegetables more interesting, we made a dressing (from

Bidding for fish at Brixham Market, principal source of south Devon fish.

Mrs Fisher) of white wine, lemon juice, butter and tabasco boiled fast together. Another accompaniment was chopped raw tomato, peeled and deseeded, with parsley and chives, vinegar and good seasoning. Such a concoction makes a good companion to many cold things – amusing too made with yellow tomatoes so that no one knows what they are eating. This is a time when a fruit vinegar comes into its own. Another adjunct was from Nathalie Hambro, made by frying chicken livers with garlic in olive oil, blending them with hard boiled eggs, a grain mustard and sherry vinegar and adding some more oil. Seasoned with green peppercorns and salt, it is served cold. [1983]

We bought a good supply of Kentish Morello cherries. This variety is not grown locally, yet it is virtually the only decent culinary sort. We have pickled some for the winter. Other uses have been in pancakes; with duck breasts; poached in brandy to accompany a loganberry, raspberry and rose petal *bombe*; and in a *bombe* itself. [1982]

The new varieties of redcurrant, for example Van Tet, have been as welcome this year as they were last (*see* my comments in the July Diary). Stone fruits have been a disaster at home, however. Our plum tree has failed. There have been some sweet smelling, but moderate tasting, greengages. We look forward to an autumn filled with apples. The first English eaters we have bought, Discovery and George Cave, were enjoyable and appalling respectively. The second had an extremely woolly texture and a strangely perfumed taste. [1983]

Capton Fruit Farm has produced first-rate baby beetroot, French beans and Desirée potatoes. Another good waxy variety that we have taken is Estima. They have had so much dill that we have been able to do a *gravlax* for the first time. Their Florentine fennel has not bulbed out this year, rather it has gone to seed. A further small crop of artichokes is coming in. There was an abrupt end to the strawberries here, although Kentish ones have been available to those who had to have them, at a price. The crops of Leveller gooseberries have been impressive. We soaked them in Muscat de Beaumes de Venise (as in Jane Grigson's *Good Things*, 1971), utterly delicious, especially if the berries are extremely ripe – a lighter flavour than if elderflower were used. Last year's harvest of this variety was spoiled by storms. They have so much more to offer than the green gooseberries of the beginning of the summer. [1982]

Potatoes seem to give us trouble at this time of year. We begin to find, especially with the shop-bought ones, that they break up after a very short time in the boiling pan. Experiment with varieties did give us Wilja, a firm waxy yellow potato that was satisfactory, as well as a Maris Bard from a specific grower who seemed to have a very good crop, but the same variety from other growers has been dreadful. These were used at the Tall Ships. At the Carved Angel we have had fewer problems with Desirée and Pentland Javelin from Capton. David Lloyd speculates that he was fortunate to have planted his maincrop early – in mid-March. Those who left it until later can expect very light yields. [1983]

For the first time there has been a glut of lobster. Prices are lower than for five years. A skin diver did confirm that in Start Bay there are more lobsters and fewer crabs in evidence. Crab has continued to be difficult. There have been days when only lobster is available. Some crabs have been brought up from Cornwall. Our unexpected delivery has been regular supplies of crayfish. The boat that has brought them has continued to work waters off the Channel Islands. Normally, they would expect to come closer to Dartmouth for the summer months but, with crab relatively scarce, they have remained on deeper ground. On this stretch there are more crayfish. During the winter the boat would expect to land in France, thus we never see them. However, in the summer the entire French fleet is at work and will not brook competition, so the Dartmouth boat brings its catch across to Brixham.

The last day of the salmon season on the Dart is August 16th. Though more fish have been caught in the last fortnight, there was a long period of complete blank and the year has never seen a glut or reduction in price except for a few days at the end of May. We were even taking fish from Scotland at the beginning of July. The fishermen talk darkly of the salmon being taken at sea. Yields of sea bass have also been low, until the last few days. There was one day when we were offered two nine pound fish by anglers. Flat fish have been more satisfactory: turbot, brill, monk, John Dory and soles have been plentiful.

We have been finding the practices of the local smokers leave a lot to be desired. We occasionally have salmon and cod's roe from Billingsgate and find the London product vastly superior to anything we can get here. It would appear that either too much dye is used or the smoke is too hot. Even smoked mackerel, local speciality this, has to be chosen with utmost care. London prices are far greater than Dartmouth's so one has to be sure to use it all, first as smoked salmon *tout court*, the trimmings being turned into a mousse and the skin going into a soup, or being fried in strips as an appetiser.

We have also been taking Dublin Bay prawns (scampi), landed at Newlyn from trawlers working the sea south of Ireland. They are packed in ice on the boats and driven at full speed to the destination. However, because of the supply chain, it is almost impossible to get them in the pink of condition. Their problems remind one that fish does go through many hands before landing on the stove. Mere purchase at market is no guarantee that it will be perfectly fresh. It depends on the boat. We can detect palpable differences in fish that comes direct from fishermen in Dartmouth and that which comes from Brixham. John Glassbrook, the fishmonger, comes back from market in despair because the fish offered for sale that morning has been left in the well of a boat with insufficient protection from the sun. No variety displays this problem so well as cod. One day perfect, another day old, probably off a deep sea boat. [1982]

Sport anglers visit us with their special prizes – too large to cook for their tea. We have been blessed with three or four large turbot this year. Bleeding these heavier fish causes reflection on the specious logic of the Christian churches in allowing their consumption on fast days. To bleed a turbot, the simplest thing is to chop the tail off and hang it in the yard for a couple of hours. When this is done, the blood literally spurts out – good red blood too, even if cold. And, of course, gutting the animal shows the same organs and mess as any mammal. Charles Lamb talks of anglers as 'patient tyrants, meek inflictors of pangs intolerable, cool devils.' One should not forget the pain with fish. [1983]

We have been pleased to find some young block Parmesan cheese at the Delicatessen. The usual material available is from a lorry that period-ically visits Dartmouth. This has dried out too much, thus has a strength and bitterness that is not ideal. Parmesan should have a nutty and warm taste and should not be so hard that it cannot be cut. Then it is too enjoyable to use in cooked dishes alone and should be eaten as part of the cheeseboard. [1983]

SALMON IN THE RIVER DART

Upstream and downstream, the river's closed.
Summer wastes in the pools.
A sunken calendar unfurls,
Fruit ripening as petals rot.

A holed-up gangster,
He dozes, his head on the same stone,
Gazing towards the skylight,
Waiting for time to run out on him.
    Ted Hughes, 'An August Salmon', from *River* (1983)

Salmon have ever caught the imagination: the spawning, the exodus, the return. Here seems a noble life of strenuous adventure. Great size allied to matchless flavour; the combination is unbeatable.

The Dart has long been a salmon river. Daniel Defoe described catching the fish at the bridge and mill race at Totnes in 1724:

We were carried hither at low water, where we saw about fifty or sixty small salmon, about seventeen to twenty inches long, which the country people call salmon-peal; and to catch these the person who went with us, who was our landlord at a great inn next the bridge, put in a net on a hoop at the end of a pole, the pole going cross the hoop at the end of the pole (which we call in this country a shove-net). The net being fixed at one end of the place, they put in a dog (who was taught his trade beforehand) at the other end of the place, and he drives all the fish into the net; so that, only holding the net still in its place, the men took up two or three and thirty salmon-peal at the first time.

Of these we had six for our dinner, for which they asked a shilling (viz., twopence a-piece); and for such fish, not at all bigger, and not so fresh, I have seen 6s. 6d. each given at a London fish-market, whither they are sometimes brought from Chichester by land-carriage. This excessive plenty of so good fish (and other provisions being likewise very cheap in proportion) makes the town of Totnes a very good place to live in; especially for such as have large families and but small estates. And many are said to come into those parts on purpose for saving money, and to live in proportion to their income.

In the Domesday survey of 1086 two fisheries are recorded at Ashprington and an annual rent of 30 salmon from the fishery of

Cornworthy, two villages below Totnes. At Dartington, up-river from that town, two fishermen paid 80 salmon in rent. Observe that the only rents in kind were salmon, otherwise the fisheries paid money. 'Fisheries' probably indicated fixed structures of some kind: weirs, staked nets, traps. The foundation documents of Totnes Priory record the gift in 1088 of a sluice or weir for fishing opposite the town, as well as of the produce of each Saturday's fishing at Judhael's fisheries at Ashprington and Cornworthy.

So it has gone on for centuries. In many parts of Devon, not only inland, salmon was the commonest form of summer fish. William Marshall, making his report on the rural economy of the south-west in 1796, observed that at Bideford market there was salmon 'in considerable plenty; but no sea fish!' The diarist William Holland, vicar of Over Stowey in the Quantock hills in Somerset, noted in 1803, 'For dinner we had some fish which is no very common thing now. I remember when fish used to be brought every other day [by the fish wives or hawkers]. Salmon at Bridgewater at two shillings per pound. I remember it at fourpence and scarce ever above sixpence.'

There exists an account of salmon fishing before the last war by Sam Cox, a resident of Tuckenhay, a small village to the north of Dartmouth. It describes graphically the techniques followed by the netsmen of the lower part of our river.

We used to go scraping for cockles at low tide, on the sandbank at the mouth of Bow Creek. It was there, in mid-channel, that the sand barge used to dredge. It was owned by Mr Baker of Stoke Gabriel, and was like a small fishing trawler . . .

Stoke Gabriel, across the river from the mouth of the stream, has been the fishing centre for as long as I can remember. In my youth, there used to be twelve to twenty boats that used to fish in the favourite haunts by the sandbank at the mouth of Bow Creek, at Duncannon, at Bass Rock, around by Sharpham, Galmpton and Cornworthy Weir.

There used to be three to four men to each boat. One man would pull the oars, another would throw out the net, whilst the third (and fourth) would remain on the foreshore. But it was possible to do it with two men, by driving a stake into the shore and knotting the ends of the rope to it, playing out the nets and then having one man pull at both ends. There were thirty to forty yards of rope, top and bottom, and the shoreman would keep hold of the ends. He had to be careful to keep one hand close to the ground, because otherwise the fish would escape underneath the net. That was the first thing they told me, when I went fishing. So the foreshoreman would hold this rope and would draw it slowly in, while the boatmen made a twenty to thirty yard semicircle from shore back to shore.

The net had cork floats on the top and lead weights on the bottom. The idea was to play it out, so that it hung straight in the water, just like a round fence. They could tell if they had caught any fish because the corks would go up and down. Each haul took roughly twenty minutes – five minutes to go around and at least fifteen minutes to pull it in. The highest number of fish I ever heard of in one haul was sixty five. When the net was in, a man would run to the boat and pull out a 'knapper'. This was a piece of round headed wood that they used to tap the fish on the head. When the haul was finished, the net was reloaded, making sure it wasn't tangled, nor fouled with sticks. Although they didn't make their own nets, the men carried out their own repairs, mainly in Stoke Gabriel, although there is still a place here in Tuckenhay. They used rails, about twenty feet long and 3 to 4 feet high and threw the net over these. Then they would pull it towards them, mending as they went.

As for the tides, low tide was no good, as they couldn't get out into the mainstream. Nor was fishing possible on a high spring tide. On these occasions the men would come up to the pub and wait for a couple of hours. They used to sit on the bank with their boats drawn up on the shore. One man might look downstream, the other two up river. They knew if a salmon was coming because it would make a trickle along the surface. Then they would say, 'He's coming' and, if the tide was right, they would run to their boats, go out and cast. If more than one boat was drawn up, they took it in turns. They didn't only catch salmon. They caught flounders, eel, bass, mullet and sprats too. Of course, the smaller net was needed for the sprats.

The season was from mid March to mid August. The week was from 6 a.m. Monday to 6 a.m. Saturday. Fishing was not allowed between then and Monday morning. Out of season, the salmon fishermen would do odd jobs, corn harvesting, digging potatoes, pulling mangolds and turnips.

I used to like going down to watch them. In fact, I used to spend hours down there, nearly always on the Ashprington side.

(*Dartington Rural Archives*, Yesterday's Village, 1978)

Conversation with a present-day fisherman confirms the facts presented above. Patrick Keene lives in Dittisham. He has been bringing salmon and other fish to us for many years. Our first encounter, and at 6' 4" it tends to be memorable, was on the quay at Brixham where, aided by a monkey, he was taking trippers' portraits. He has held a salmon netting licence for the last four years, together with eighteen other boats working this stretch of the river. Two of them come from Dittisham, one from Tuckenhay and one from Totnes, but the majority are based at Stoke Gabriel on the other side of the river. A couple of licences are held by absentee owners who let their boats out to local operators. No one fishes alone; it is possible with two, the norm is three, sometimes four. The proceeds of the catch are shared; a blank day is truly blank for all parties. These days may repeat, occasionally for as long as a month on end. The days of the great hauls are over. The most Patrick has caught in one cast of the net is 13 fish; the best in the last six years on the river has been 36 fish; the best ever, 62 fish in 1922.

The causes of the decline in numbers have been widely canvassed. Patrick would put much of it down to the Greenland fishery. Salmon are taken at sea in monofilament nets of immense length, perhaps two miles. Vast catches are recorded. The Greenland season is short – two weeks – but the damage is great. If you add to that the predations of the Irish boats as the salmon round southern Ireland and the activities of the poachers, little wonder that stocks appear reduced, without thinking of the diseases, pollution and dams. The sport fisherman, casting his fly in a stratagem to lure the salmon to take the hook, will roundly condemn the netsmen, no skill, no chance for the salmon, stopping the fish before they have even got upstream, taking too many out of the water, and so on. The debate will continue as long as the imbalance remains, and the original cause will never be established to the satisfaction of all.

Today's nets are made of nylon twine, not monofilament. They are seine nets with a permitted length of 180 yards although normally they are no more than 120. They have a top rope, with cork floats, and a weighted bottom rope. The net between the ropes is so shaped that it does not hang as a curtain but will, when drawn in, form a pocket or 'bunt' at its middle point. This acts like a cod-end in a trawl net. Regulations state that a haul must start on the river bank and must finish there too. The routine is that one man stands on the bank holding the top and bottom ropes of the net. The boat casts off and pays out the net in an approximate semi-circle, coming ashore some 50 yards down stream from the anchor man. He then walks up to the landing place and the net is hauled in, the weighted bottom rope ensuring that the fish do not escape. As the net is brought closer to the shore so the 'bunt' is formed by the fish trying to swim outwards. When the net is entirely beached, the 'napper' is brought out of the boat and each fish is dispatched by a bop on the head just behind the eyes. It is considered bad luck to produce the napper before the fish are ashore.

The skill in netting lies in knowing the habits of the fish in varying conditions. It also helps if you know the state of the river bed. In the reaches around Stoke Gabriel there is a lot of rubbish from the Second World War impeding the bottom rope of any net cast improvidently on the water. Similarly, old yacht moorings cause much trouble for beneath each tiny orange buoy lies a great hunk of concrete and old iron. The Dittisham fishermen have been protesting at the expansion of yacht moorings across customary hauls; they have accounted for nearly half of the traditional spots on the Dittisham side. It is now the rule that the Harbour Authority maps and protects such sites from further invasion.

The reason for wanting hauls on the west bank of the river, even though the majority are on the other side, is that when the wind is hard south west or westerly the salmon prefer to stay in the lee. Preservation of the Dittisham sites is thus imperative for constant working throughout the season. Salmon appear to go upstream by following the scent of fresh water. It is thus axiomatic that if the river is in flood they will race through the fresh water and achieve the upper reaches, where the rods are waiting, before the netsmen have a chance. This is one reason for our not having had good early seasons in late years – the springs have been too wet. In 1984, fish were being caught at Dartmeet on the moor with the sea lice still on them, so rapid had their transit through tidal waters been. 1976 was a good year for salmon in Dartmouth because the long dry summer left the fish ambling round the pool at Stoke Gabriel waiting for signs of fresh water from the moor. The fact that salmon commonly swim against the current means that their behaviour may depend on whether the tide is on the ebb or flood. It is possible to catch them swimming apparently downstream because an eddy or whirlpool has fooled them into thinking that this is the way to go. The river is deceptive to the eye of the fisherman as well. One of the best spots is actually in the widest part of the stream. You would think that the fish would have the whole breadth (more than a mile) to choose from, but they swim along narrow corridors created out of currents and subaqueous contours.

The routine of fishing depends on the season as well as the day to day conditions. As most fishermen have other, daytime, jobs, they will mostly spend the evenings on the river. At the beginning of the season, in March, they are often loath to occupy several cold and wet hours on the off chance of a catch. It is rare that a crew will squander their energy on aimless casting of the net. They need some indication that success may lurk below. During the spring and early summer this may be no more than an informed assessment of the weather and the tides. As the year progresses, the fish begin to behave differently, jumping out of the water as they go, and a more canny approach is adopted. The crew will loll on the banks until a jumper is espied. 'There 'e was' is the customary call to action as they run to put the net out – on the assumption that where one fish has jumped others may be passing. Believe it or not, this works.

The time for the largest fish is the spring. The giants (20lb plus) may swim through in the winter. Usually the August fish are smaller. In Dittisham they are called 'harvestmen', in Stoke Gabriel 'lammies' (?after Lammas). The sea trout or 'truff' (the general Dart name) also follows this pattern.

The rivers of south Devon are not especially prolific of salmon. This may account for the relatively high price we pay – at least 25 per cent above the Scottish. Salmon trout will always be 20 per cent cheaper – unjustifiably in my view, for eating that is. When buying from the boats, one has a reasonable amount of time to make a sale before condition declines. There is a lead-in period of up to four days, depending on size and the period spent out of refrigeration in the hands of the fishermen, before the stiffness has gone out of the body and the flesh completely relaxed. This makes it a safer fish to buy than, say, John Dory or brill. We will gut as soon as the fish is brought to us, usually through the gills rather than making a long slit down the stomach. This leaves the stomach lining intact and makes for tidier steak, if you are cutting in this fashion. The line of clotted blood along the backbone can be removed from each steak before cooking.

By far the majority of the salmon brought to us is served as steaks. These are cut from the fish, across the backbone, and cooked in a small copper flat on the top of the stove with a little butter, turning it once to seal it but without letting it take colour. A little wine is added and the flat is covered with aluminium foil. We may then give it four minutes in the hot oven 200–230°C / 400–450°F / gas mark 7 before transferring it to the cool oven 110°C / 225°F / gas mark ¼ for a further ten or fifteen minutes before it is needed. If there is a long run in to service, the steak can be cooked in the cool oven throughout. This method is not intended to substitute for a grilled or fried cut where the taste of the butter and some colour from the cooking should be expected. These steaks will normally be presented with a *hollandaise* sauce, or a sorrel *hollandaise*. A good alternative has been using champagne as the liquid at the beginning of the cooking, which is then reduced with cream at the end before pouring over the steak. Another variation was to add mushrooms and red wine at the beginning and reducing this and finishing it with butter at the end.

If we have a lot of fish, or a big one, then we may offer it in two ways: as steaks and in pastry with ginger and currants. This latter recipe, a speciality of the Hole in the Wall in Bath, is most popular. It is also an economical way of dealing with tails and shoulders, as well as making fish at the end of the season more palatable. With the onset of full breeding conditions, the males get a pronounced hook to the jaw, the skin gets tougher and the flesh drier. One day a fish in just this state was brought in to us, but it was offered not as a salmon but as a grayling – a species in the salmon family but living entirely in fresh water and not growing larger than two or three pounds. Our fishmonger remembered fish of just this sort being delivered him from Berwick on Tweed at the end of the summer and being called grayling.

If we have small pieces of salmon to use after devoting the major part of it to main courses, the most frequent recipes are a *ceviche*, a salmon mousse or a salmon and lobster mousse, salmon and mushroom cutlets and *hure de saumon* – a Michel Guérard specific for salmon in aspic with green peppercorns, hard boiled egg, lemon and pimento.

September

Not relevant, but the Carved Angel maintained its lead over Dartmouth restaurants when our representative, David Mills, won the Royal Regatta waiters' race in fine style. [1982]

We had a good Regatta in Dartmouth. The weather was exceptional. Our record in the waiters' race was not maintained – David Mills, visiting us for a second summer's punishment, finished first, with a stupendous sprint, but regrettably he had spilled more beer from his glass than the contestant who finished last. As the race is sponsored by a brewery, the beer was the measure not the running. [1983]

Rowanberries have been made into a jelly with a cheese from the pulp. The latter was too dry tasting to be palatable. A second basketful contained riper fruit and the jelly from that is much better. Wild rosehips have come in for a jelly made with apple. Chanterelles continue quite regularly at present although no one has come in with plain field mushrooms, perhaps too early and too dry. [1982]

David Beazley has brought a good haul of chanterelles and two sorts of *boletus* from Dartmoor. The first were in excellent condition, did not give off the immense amount of moisture that they sometimes do. One answer is to grill them for a minute or two to drive off the moisture. One can see why they are so much more expensive than other sorts of mushroom. Even a small quantity pervades a dish with its taste and smell. We also have had some field mushrooms from various people. The rain must have brought them on. It is said the harvest is very large this year. [1983]

The fields have been covered with mushrooms. David Beazley brought us an example of *Leucopaxillus Giganteus* (he said) which resembled a cep. It was firm in texture, with a peppery taste although we found it slightly bitter. On our visit to France earlier this month, ceps abounded,

Domestic livestock at Allaleigh, 1986.

best eaten *à la bordelaise* at Claude Darroze at Langon in Sauternes country. We are in two minds about wild mushrooms at the moment. They figure widely on restaurant menus. Often we find the taste disappointing; unable to stand up to the cream in their sauce; sometimes a little musty; just boring. [1984]

From Stokely Barton Fruit Farm, five miles south of Dartmouth, we have had marionberries, a cross between a blackberry and loganberry. They look like very dark loganberries, but the blackberry flavour predominates. They make a good ice cream. We have never had so many blackberries as this year. Strawberries have ceased to be picked locally, although Taunton vale is still harvesting. Their crops have a sweetness and intensity better than any other time this year. Autumn raspberries have benefited from the excellent weather at Dittisham Fruit Farm, improving all the while in appearance and flavour. Zeva are still being picked and Sceptre, which are similar, have begun. They also have September, a small round berry with a very sweet taste and Delight, a large berry, quite light in colour with a sharper flavour. If the weather holds, the latest variety, Heritage, will be cropping in October. [1981]

Although citrus fruits have been in the doldrums of late – we have been charged more for lemons than ever before and the oranges have been of low quality – yet a few tangerines (not Minneolas which are not worth the trouble) have been large and first class. The English tree fruits have been getting very interesting. Worcester Pearmains were of crisp texture, large size and zestful perfume. We have also had some Kentish Cox's. These seem quite early for this variety and of a different colour from that which we are used to. However, once through the firm skin, there is a very crisp and juicy interior with a great deal of acidity. Mr and Mrs Peter Wheldon brought us some Merton Pride pears from Suffolk. These were of perfect conformation, with a wonderful balance of fruit and flavour. It has been grand to watch them turn from a dull green/brown to a glowing golden orange over two weeks. [1983]

We have had sugar peas this autumn. At first we started to shell them for they looked like small garden peas. Noticing, however, that the pod was fleshier than usual and the pea smaller, we took to stringing them and cooking them whole. They are extremely sweet and succulent. A second picking was delivered in the second half of September. This is the latest we have had peas grown in this district. [1981]

We had a certain interruption of supplies of lemon soles due to the ruining of the ground by big beamer trawlers scalloping over it. Scallops are fished by use of a dredge, this has the effect of ploughing the sea bed. While undertaking this process off Start Point, the trawlers uprooted lengths of disused telephone cable. These are now waving in the water ready to foul Mike Lynn's smaller trawls. He estimates that the ground will not return to its former self for at least six months. What is so silly about this episode is that the scallops are not worth eating at the moment. [1983]

Mr Distin was observing that crab caught in shallow water is better than deep sea produce. When feeling ill, or wounded, their tendency is to retreat to the deep, thus giving rise to watery flesh, poor brown meat, etc. [1982]

We have taken salted silverside from three different butchers in recent weeks. Two of them did not brine it for long enough; one of them put the odds and ends in the pickle (those which had not been sold on Saturday) so that they were unsatisfactory joints; but one, Russell's, produces an impeccable piece of meat, brined correctly. [1982]

Mrs Shillabeer's chickens have been developing well and giving much pleasure. The group that is being fed a diet of maize is now eight weeks old. They are not putting on the sort of weight that would be expected. They apparently dislike maize, only resorting to it once the other ingredients of their feed have been consumed. [1981]

RABBITS

Rabbit is often included in our menus. It comes wild, either shot or snared, or bred specifically for the table. It offers variety of meat and at one time seemed better than unsatisfactory chicken. It is not, however, without its own problems. When supplied from the wild, it can be dry and tough. Such deficiencies are insupportable when the taste is not enough to offer as a counter attraction. Farm-bred rabbits do not suffer from that, but they are sometimes insipid and their texture, especially in stews and *fricassées*, may tend to the shiny or slimy (depending on how you look at it). They do need to be of a decent size, otherwise the ratio of flesh to bone is too small on the lesser joints and the eater is for ever disentangling the one from the other. These are not free-range animals. They are fed with rabbit nuts and hay and kept indoors in cages. They are similar, therefore, to the continental rabbits seen in every house's back yard. They have no connection with gaminess at all. A pet I remember with fondness was a black doe that lived in the back garden. Providentially, this was an area quite impossible to exit from as well as being free of predators. The rabbit had the time of her life, excavating subterranean palaces, eating every plant that took her fancy and beating off or playing with the house cat. The toll of plants was eventually so great that the tax was deemed excessive and she was sent to live with a buck in the country. When liberated from her urban fastness, she promptly grew twofold and developed a savage and uncontrollable temper. She was last heard of breaking out to freedom in the fields.

Our source for these animals is Mr Turner of Hansel, Stoke Fleming. He has nine breeding does and one buck of New Zealand White variety. These give him a crop of about ten animals per week. Each doe has a litter every six weeks of between eight and ten kittens. Over the next two months to ten weeks they grow to five pounds live weight at which point they are killed, giving between three and three and a half pounds in the pot. With this number of rabbits, Mr Turner has few problems with disease. When he had 55 breeding does, he found that there were constant respiratory and stomachic infections to which they are susceptible when kept indoors. Mr Turner also found it difficult to dispose of the meat produced on this scale for there is a restricted market since the days of myxomatosis. The Turners call it the 'Watership Down Syndrome'. Much excess production is exported, thus breeders, who operate anyway on fine margins, are vulnerable to fluctuations in exchange rates. Mr Turner may dispose of any surplus to a Lincolnshire firm which exports to Belgium. Their price is very low, so this is a last resort. Other outlets are to local butchers, direct sales in weekly markets or to restaurants.

Mr Turner's record system is majestic in its efficiency and detail. We had a small problem with one of his animals – it was not as tender as expected. He was able to tell immediately from which litter it had come, when it was killed and everything else about its life history worthy of remark. Control is necessary to know when a doe is ready for mating, about to give birth, etc., so that these events, when correctly anticipated, do not cause undue distress.

Baked rabbit with spring onions

1 rabbit	2 bunches spring onions
Thyme, marjoram, parsley	4oz / 110g streaky bacon rashers
1 lemon	5fl oz / 150ml chicken stock
2fl oz / 60ml olive oil	5fl oz / 150ml dry white wine
2oz / 50g butter	

The rabbit, if wild, wants to be young and tender. This dish is a serious error if the meat is tough. Many people would aver that the wild animal has the more interesting flavour; however, it can be argued that the combination of tenderness and extra flesh more than compensates for any lack in the hutch-reared rabbit. Baking or roasting gives texture that does not come from a casserole; marinating gives depth of flavour.

Cut the rabbit into joints: the hind legs, two or three pieces of saddle (loin), and the shoulders. The latter can be taken off most of the rib bones so as to minimise the number of small bones for eating. Wild rabbit bones tend to splinter more than do those of tame stock. Care should therefore be taken to sever at the joints and not to shatter the bones with too large and blunt an instrument – a large sharp knife with steady pressure is the best.

Place the joints in a marinade overnight. This is made by chopping the herbs, grating the rind and squeezing the lemon and mixing with black pepper and olive oil.

Take the joints out of the marinade, season them and dust with a little flour. Fry them, turning once or twice, in butter in a *sauté* pan. Chop the spring onions into 2in / 5cm lengths, discarding the coarsest green parts, add them to the pan. Then cover the joints with short lengths of rinded streaky bacon. Put on a tight fitting lid and bake in the oven preheated to 200°C / 400°F / gas mark 6 for 15 minutes. Check that it is cooked, the best joint for testing being the hind leg, using the same method as for chicken. Place the rabbit and trimmings on a serving dish to keep warm and add to the pan the stock and white wine. Reduce by half through boiling. Check the seasoning and add to the rabbit.

This extremely simple dish can be the best way to eat the animal. Ideally the marinade will have imparted just the right amount of flavour to give it interest without completely overpowering the mild taste of the rabbit itself.

Rabbit cooked with leeks and mustard

1 rabbit	10fl oz / 300ml chicken stock
4oz / 110g streaky bacon in the piece	½oz / 15g flour
2oz / 50g butter	5fl oz / 150ml dry white wine
2 yolks of egg	1 dessertspoonful strong Dijon mustard
5fl oz / 150 ml double cream	Thyme, marjoram, 1 lemon,
1lb / 450g trimmed leeks	olive oil for the marinade

Joint and marinate the rabbit as in the preceding recipe, but exclude the parsley and the grated rind of the lemon.

Dice the bacon and melt in a casserole with the butter. Add the prepared leeks, cut into 1in / 2.5cm lengths. Fry gently for about three minutes. Remove the bacon and leeks and replace with the seasoned joints of the rabbit. Brown them lightly and then remove them to join the leeks and bacon. Sprinkle in the flour, add the stock and wine slowly and make a light *roux*, stirring the while. Season this sauce. Replace the bacon, leeks and rabbit, cover and cook in a very slow oven until just tender – about three quarters of an hour.

In a small bowl, make a beaten *liaison* of the egg yolks, cream and mustard. When you are ready to serve the dish, pour this into the casserole. Shuffle it gently, without allowing it to boil, until the sauce is thickened. Check the seasoning.

The danger of this recipe is that it is insipid. The flavour of tame rabbit is not great; wild animals may therefore be preferred. Tame rabbit can also have a pappy texture when casseroled. If there is not enough mustard or seasoning, or if you serve too much sauce with the meat, you will have a dish that tastes quite nice but lacks attack.

Both these dishes are adorned by sippets of fried bread on which are spread the chopped and fried liver, kidney and heart of the rabbits.

Rabbit terrine

If you only like joints with a lot of meat on them, it may be a solution to use the saddle and hindquarters in a roast and the rest of the carcase in a terrine

1lb / 450g boned rabbit meat	2fl oz / 60ml white wine
1lb / 450g fat belly pork	1 clove garlic
1fl oz / 30ml brandy	1 bunch parsley
The liver of the rabbit	1 sprig of thyme
2oz / 50g streaky bacon	Streaky bacon to line the terrine

Bone the rabbit and skin the belly pork. Cut half a pound of each into thin strips and marinate with the brandy for two hours. Mince the rest of the rabbit and pork with the liver, bacon, garlic, parsley and thyme. Season well and mix with the white wine. Line a terrine with streaky bacon rashers, without their rind, and fill with alternate layers of the marinated meats and the farce, finishing with the latter. Cover with foil and cook in a slow oven 130°C / 250°F / gas mark ½ in a water bath. This will take between one and one and a half hours. It will be cooked when a skewer thrust into the centre reveals clear rather than pink liquid. Cool and press lightly. Serve the following day, with spiced fruit, gherkins and a salad.

A good terrine, with a fresh taste and not too strong. The pork specified here has not been salted, but if it is left in a brine for a day or two the flavour helps avoid any insipidity. However, this will depend on the butcher; rare is the household that has a brine tub at the ready. It is also possible to mix a large handful of sorrel leaves with the farce meat before it goes through the mincer. This gives an amusing colour as well as some acidity.

October

The last weeks have been dominated by storms and tempests. Hopes of an Indian summer proved evanescent, affecting the continuity of vegetables and soft fruit as well as restricting the choice of fish on the market. The weather notwithstanding, Mrs Lloyd has been able to bring in a few raspberries and Mr Rogers has had a small quantity of late strawberries, some of good flavour, others too watery to eat on their own. Green vegetables have been better than we dared hope. We began the month with further pickings of peas from Mr Rogers. He began cropping half way through June and the last came to us on September 25th. The later pickings lacked the piercing sweetness of the first. He has also had some late broad beans. They were all right so long as each bean was skinned before being tossed in butter and cream. Calabrese has been consistent and of good flavour during the last fortnight as has been spinach. Our potatoes have got better. We have been having very large Desirée from Mr Rogers, waxy enough to boil without breaking up, yet have made good creamed potato and *gratin dauphinois*. It is lucky to get a tuber that will do all three without complaint. [1981]

Green vegetables have gone through the death throes of summer and moved firmly towards autumn. Courgettes from Admiral Haynes regained their earlier form, however, and some small late runner beans proved excellent eating with pesto. Good tomatoes continue for the time being, but cucumber pickle is the order of the day. Spinach has been coming from Slapton and retains its flavour even though being tougher than usual, needing longer cooking. Leeks are of fine flavour and condition and good celeriac has started again. Mr Rogers' watercress is back in production after its flowering and is, as ever, better than the commercially distributed cress, if only because it is picked to order. He has also been able to continue with Webbs lettuce. The problems of producing this variety all the year round have been overcome. Even when under glass, it is far better than the winter alternatives of Chinese

Two goatlings, Anglo-Nubian/Toggenburg cross.

leaves or iceberg lettuce. The next step for him, one may hope, is to try growing cos and, perhaps, curly endives. [1982]

A subscriber brought us back a spice mixture from Spain *para pinchitos* – for small kebabs. Made with salt, chilli, garlic, cumin and coriander, such things are intriguing both as a means of bringing out flavours (the use of coriander with carrot) and as tastes in their own right. Large doses of chilli do give added energy at the end of a long night as well as making a small quantity of food go further. They have a way of making a meal more of a heart-stopping event that must have recommended them to generations of the ill-fed. The next step, of refinement and sophistication, is the product of plenty. [1983]

Autumn brings its fruits too. We have had Mr Bartlett's muscatel grapes from Strete – incomparable flavour, the only way to make chicken Véronique. Joyce Molyneux has also picked her quinces. A good crop, though she tried in vain to grow one in a bottle for a quince ratafia. She has made some quince cheese and some jelly, sharpened with vinegar. Apples too are coming in. We found Spartan this month. It has the crispness of a Granny Smith and the flavour of a Cox's. It has an intense acidity that is finally outweighed by the fruit, thus rather exciting to eat. Peter Wheldon has posted us his selection for our October Dinner: Spartan, which he describes as a cross between Mackintosh and Yellow Newton introduced from British Columbia twenty years ago; Greensleeves, an apple bred recently at East Malling from James Grieve and Golden Delicious; and Egremont Russet. [1983]

In the garden we have sewn some lambs' leaves (*mâche*) to give us winter salads. We bought four varieties when last in France: *verte de Cambrai, vert à coeur plein, grosse graine d'Hollande (doucette)* and *coquille de Louviers*. They have all germinated, along with some land cress. [1981]

Bad weather, says Mr Distin, is good for prawn fishing. He gave us the benefit of his thoughts the other day, contradicting our idea that prawns are lured to pots by foetid bait. He maintains that they are washed out of their lairs in rock and sand (the sand-dwellers have a different coloration when alive – milkier, less transparent) by high seas. They grasp any port in the storm; if we are lucky, a crab or prawn pot. He notes that most of them are attached to the funnels of the crab pots when they are hauled, not feeding at all. The upshot was that he had put his own prawn traps on new ground a little further from the shoreline, having failed signally in their previous location. The results were dramatic. Daily visits with two or three pounds have been the rule. [1983]

The poultry thrive in the care of Mrs Shillabeer. Those mainly fed on maize have arrived in the kitchen. They did not approve of their maize diet, although Mrs Shillabeer observes that her layers seem quite to like it. The birds were appreciably smaller than the normally fed ones. They lack the distinctive colour of many of the French corn-fed birds, which comes from breed not feed as might be inferred from their bright corn yellow. The flesh was very moist, no hint of that rubberiness that sometimes worries. The breast meat was quite white. The flavour was excellent but not markedly better than the other birds from Dittiscombe farm. [1981]

We finished the Manx lamb that we had bought for a Middle Eastern dinner. We felt that the cous-cous dish was the best way we cooked it: the strength of the apricots and other flavours balancing the tastiness of the lamb. We did much of the prime meat on skewers and charcoal grill, marinating the meat in small pieces. The flavour was very pronounced and I found this extremely enjoyable. There was a term to the development of flavour after hanging, moving from good to intrusive as the last pieces were cooked for our supper. The texture was firm, too firm some would say, and not made much less so by marinating. However, a worthwhile experiment that made us look forward to the new season's lambs from the rare breeds farms in North Devon. At the same time, we took quite a lot of English lamb from Luscombe of Totnes and, although late in the season, this was still of excellent quality. [1982]

We bought a new goats' cheese, made by Mrs N. J. Kent of Capton. (We have since become the owners of two of her kids.) A hard cheese, from Anglo-Nubians and Toggenburgs, the latter having a lower fat content. The cheese, about 2lb weight, has matured a month. She would reckon it to have another month's life. It is very mild, with good texture without being too crumbly, strongly resembling feta to taste. [1983]

TABOO FOOD

A paper at the Oxford Symposium on Food and Food History in 1985 related to the eating of dogs. Even in such rarefied company of food academics and enthusiasts, the subject engendered a ripple of outrage. 'Was the man having us on, I mean, was he serious?' Nonetheless, the truism remains: westerners don't eat dogs and crazy people, like Filipinos and Chinese, do. In California, there is a society devoted to stamping out the practice in the New Empire of the American Pacific.

While the formation of taboos is a subject for psycho-ethnographers, Freud, Lévi-Strauss *et alii*, we are living through a period of rapid change in perceptions of what is and what is not permissible food. This has been charted for the centuries since the Reformation by Keith Thomas, in his *Man and the Natural World* (1983). More recently, Stephen Mennell has discussed the same question in his *All Manners of Food* (1985). As our sensibilities increased or altered and we began to take a more holistic view of the world, so humanitarianism, perhaps a contrary tendency, also took hold. Great areas became out of bounds, especially to Englishmen: dogs, cats, song birds, horses. 'What! Robins! Our household birds! I would as soon eat a child,' exclaimed Mount-stuart Elphinstone when travelling in Italy in the middle of the last century. As certain species were less palatable, so the slaughter of those that were left became less brutal. Flaying, polling, bleeding were superseded by the humane killer. We distanced the process, banished it from the shambles to the abattoir. As faith in our own after-life diminished so it dawned on many that death to an ox was the same as death to a human. Mortality being the bugbear that it now is, the question has to be answered: 'How can we kill anything?'

There are signs that increasing numbers of people would like never to kill, although that alienation that renders our society so difficult of comprehension means that millions of us are quite happy to witness death vicariously so long as the hand that wields the weapon is not ours. The result, gastronomically, is that meat itself becomes taboo or that its processing is so mechanised that we can fool ourselves that it never happened. Even hunters may avoid the consequences of their actions, so squeamish are they in the face of death. A fisherman brought us a 16lb turbot the other day which he had been unable to kill. It takes skill and dispatch to cope with it humanely. He had left it in the bottom of the boat, doubtless suffering more than it would have done had he walloped it as he caught it.

The test of our attitudes towards such taboos came with the arrival on the kitchen table of a badger. It had been caught mistakenly in a fox trap, necessitating its destruction. We took a hindquarter. None of us had eaten this meat before, though badger hams have entered the folk memory of Englishmen. 'The badger is one of the cleanest creatures, in its food, of any in the world and one may suppose that the flesh of this creature is not unwholesome. It eats like the finest pork, and is much sweeter than pork.' So writes Richard Bradley in the early eighteenth century while including a recipe from one R.T. in Leicestershire for brining the gammons before spit-roasting them. Waverley Root calls badger the food of eighteenth-century English peasants seeking more succulent fare. He is accurate in this, for it was by no means dry, and had a pronounced layer of fat over the ham. Where we differ from all those people whose written comments we could find is in comparing it to pork or sucking pig. Lilli Gore for example, in *Game Cooking* (1974), commenting on the possibility or otherwise of eating bear meat, remarks, 'After I discovered what I thought to be delicious sucking pig was in fact a badger, I decided there and then to "suspend my disbelief".' We found that the most useful comparison was to mutton. The meat was dark, succulent and strong tasting, but in no way like pork, having a particular smell to it, just as does roast leg of lamb.

The ham was not large, weighing only two pounds. However, authorities had led us to expect something from four to eight pounds. We were assured that the animal was adult – its pelt would not have made us think it was anything else. The fear was that it would be dry and tough. Therefore, the method of cooking was to lard it first with herbs (mostly thyme) and then to marinate it with red wine, bay leaf, thyme and parsley, carrots and celery. It stayed in the marinade for the best part of a week. It was then pot roasted, after browning, with the marinade in a cool oven. It took much longer to cook than so small a joint should have done, upwards of three hours. It was not overcooked as a result and, although firm, was not tough. The fat, of which there was ample, was not much enjoyed. It had not been shown the open crisping heat of a hot oven.

The most informative book on badgers is Henry Smith's *Master Book of Poultry and Game* (n.d., c.1950). This is a catch-all compendium, designed for the catering trade. He has instructions for curing and baking a ham, for a pie from the fore-quarters and for roasting the legs. The latter includes a seasoning of ginger and an accompanying sauce of horse-radish or gooseberry. He suggests making a gravy from the feet and the tail. I would like to know where he found his recipes. One has difficulty imagining a Trust House in the 1950s offering in its *table d'hôte* 'roast leg of badger with gooseberry sauce'.

The real question is whether we enjoyed the meal. I do not think we did. The taste was by no means unpleasant, although rich. However, the psychological difficulties in eating a truly wild animal weighed heavily upon us. Had we thought it some variant breed of lamb, delivered by the Rare Breeds Farm, we would have been interested and mildly enthusiastic. None of us has the stomach to consume wild things. Game birds no longer count as wild – the few that have not been hand-reared are soon included in the semi-domestic bracket by a quick elision of the facts. Venison has suffered the same process and is no longer viewed as a mere creature of the forest; has it not been emparked for centuries? So which wild beasts do we eat? We would not take squirrel, bear or otter; nor would we accept lark, thrush or blackbird. (The poser of thrush pâté is perhaps solved by the very fact that it is pâté.) Hares we do take and eat; they constitute the greatest exception. However, their kinship with rabbit (permissible vermin) acts against their interest. Even so, there is increasing evidence of people refusing hare.

Keith Thomas suggests that rejection of song birds as part of our diet was due to increasing prosperity; their capture and preparation was less productive than a turkey's. Some of our own opinions of meat are economically induced, as beef prices soar and that great complex of reasons that has governed the diets of Japan and parts of India has begun to take root here too. Ours is a dense population, cut off from the country in urban sprawl; soon there will be no room for stock rearing. Animals that have been left, totems of another life in another world, will be extensions of our psyches; consumption will be self-destruction.

November

And then he kindly gave to me
A lovely coloured booklet free.
'Twas full of prose that sang the praise
  Of coaching inns in Georgian days,
    Showing how public-houses are
    More modern than the motor-car,
  More English than the weald or wold
      And almost equally as old,
    And run for love and not for gold
      Until I felt a filthy swine
For loathing beer and liking wine.
          John Betjeman, 'The Village Inn'

As the season changes emphatically to its autumn rhythm, so do the new arrivals in the kitchen, keeping interest and enthusiasm at a high pitch. We tackle even the plucking of the first game with élan, reserving our ennui for the deep winter. [1981]

But all is not even from one year to the next.
As autumn turns to winter, the customers, save at half-terms, evaporate. A moderate sense of ease and sloth settles on the river front; there commence weeks of disappearance, not additions. [1982]

1982 was a time when anxiety had clouded our perception, even of the seasons.
We returned from Cornwall with a bag of Maris Peer potatoes that proved to be cooking much better than those, of the same variety, that were supplied in Dartmouth. They have not broken up, their flavour is mild but enjoyable, their colour is white. These had been dug and clamped in September. As has been observed before, performance is not only a matter of variety, but where and how they are grown. We had also been served some Pink Fir Apple potatoes. They are a knobbly

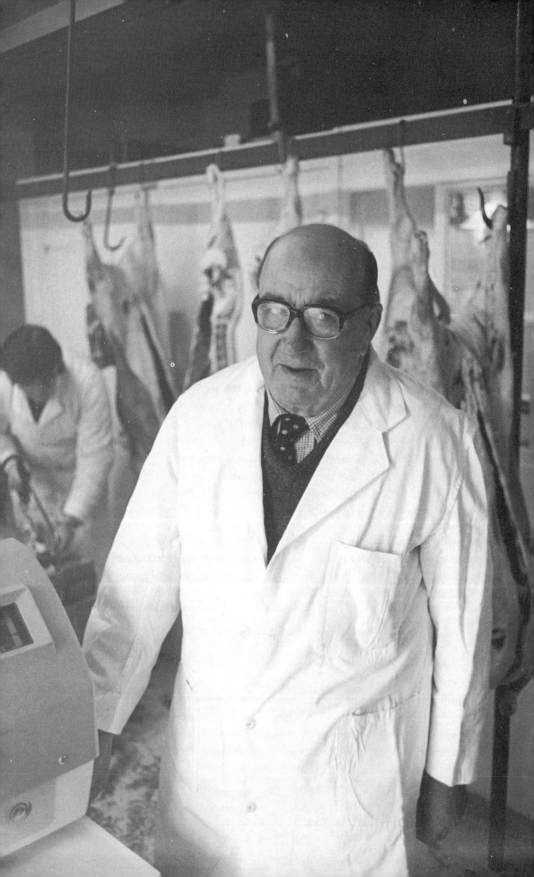

tuber, in some instances resembling Jerusalem Artichokes, that cook very densely and waxily, with a flavour that recalls new potatoes while being available through the winter months. They are usually used for salads, because they slice well and do not break up when tossed and because of their strong flavour. However, they are gaining ground as a boiling potato for restaurant use. They still cost several times the usual price of a maincrop. [1981]

In preparation for a dish to be given in the November Subscription Dinner (gratin of pumpkins, as described by Richard Olney) we requested some of the gourd from our greengrocer. In the event, he had none in the district and was forced to get some from London markets. We are, by now, expert in using up pumpkin. Most years see us inundated by embarrassed gardeners, unsure what to do now they have grown the brute. Only a small surplus in 1981, however. Eventually one came in from Kingsbridge in addition to two from London, each weighing 36 pounds. Allowing enough for the dinner, we have been able to make a purée for serving as a vegetable, a jam with ginger adapted from the marrow and ginger recipe given by the Ministry of Agriculture's book on home preserves and bottling, and a chutney with tomato taken from Elizabeth David's *Salt and Spices* (1970). [1981]

The herbs are coming to an end. The basil dressing with a goat's cheese salad was the last showing for the herb – fresh. Sorrel still grows, though the slugs may overtake it. In vegetables, we have had some first rate calabrese, although quite stalky. Economy, as well as taste, dictates that we peel the stalks and cook them separately; with a Seville orange *hollandaise* is good. French beans have been of a high standard. Red peppers still arrive from Mr Rogers' greenhouse. Spinach from Slapton has finished with the end of the month. It was fresh and good, without bitterness. We have just started using red cabbage, a sure sign of winter, trying it as detailed by Colin Spencer: apple, vinegar, cinnamon and allspice rather than the usual mixture of apple, vinegar and sugar. [1983]

We have been tasting a few of the apples sold in Dartmouth this month: a sorry show they make. Of eight varieties on sale on a single day, three were of the Delicious family: Golden, Red (from Canada) and Jonagold. Two were Cox's – one small and one large. There was a Granny Smith, a russet and a Spartan. The two with quality were Jonagold and

Albert Luscombe in his shop, Totnes.

the russet. These had sufficiently intense flavour and balance of fruit and acid, coupled with firmness of flesh. The others were insipid, lacking any variety of flavour – merely a cheap perfume – or even any taste at all, for example the Granny Smith. The Cox's were an especial disappointment. They have been degraded by the growers, in search of reliability and cropping. H. V. Taylor commented (*The Apples of England*, 1948) that the English had managed to educate 'our pomological senses to observe fine distinctions not yet realised by others'. The position then was not much better than today, many of his tasting comments in the catalogue are as uncharitable as ours might be. [1982]

We had a response to the above comment in the form of a letter from Mr Peter Levi from Oxford, recounting his experience of buying apples in the Market there and affording some perspective on our bilious remarks. Ashmead Kernels, Egremont Russets, St Cecilia, Ribstone Pippin, Worcester Pearmain, James Grieve, Tydeman's Late Orange, all came in for praise, though not without qualification, and all had been bought in the 1982 season in the one district. One is occasionally unnecessarily dismissive of apples bought in a shop. The reason may be that sharp pang of disappointment experienced as you bite into yet another woolly and characterless orb, perfection though it may appear to contain. Repeated doses engender resentment. Yet there are growers of unblemished devotion and standards; there are researchers such as Joan Morgan revitalising our understanding of varieties for both cooking and eating; the station at East Malling has done much to develop means of growth both more reliable and more successful, as well as varieties that stand up to comparison with the best of the last century. Much of the fault must lie with the marketing of these fruits. We have come to expect apples all the year round, thus we demand importation of the characterless. Our haste to consume also results in the putting on sale of fruit that is inadequately ripened – this may be the cause for the decline in standard of even the most reliable varieties such as Cox's.

We visited Beenleigh Mill, Harbertonford during the pressing of apples for cider. The operation was impressive: the gas engine chugging away; the vast press being loaded with trays of pulp; delectable apple juice; men rushing this way and that; great pipes, used for whisky, rum or sherry in their previous careers, being filled with the new cider; all in the penumbra of a November afternoon. [1982]

Prawns have started to reappear now that summer has gone. Mr Distin is catching them quite close to the shore. Although only a few at a time, he manages to bring them two or three times a week. He has also been bringing in hermit crabs. These he usually sells to anglers for bait. We had never eaten them before. However, having extracted them from their shells and boiled them for two minutes, the snail-like leathery body yields up a succulent and tasty morsel of flesh. [1981]

We visited the Helford River oyster beds at Port Navas. They are in creeks leading to the main river (which is too busy and affected by mineral workings to be entirely satisfactory) and they are farmed to a similar cycle (though longer) of sowing, growing and harvesting, of a farm on dry land. The oysters, natives, are graded according to five sizes and, surprisingly, the third and fourth sizes were held by the manager to be best for flavour. We bought a small basket, a small droplet in their output of one and a half million. Their flavour was quite salty, but the meat is plumper and more palpable than the Pacifics that we get nearer home. The oysters will not keep beyond a week after they had been lifted from their cleansing tanks scanned by ultra-violet. Long life in a bivalve is something that the Victorians took for granted more than do we. Hubert Byng Hall, in *The Oyster, where, how and when to find, breed, cook and eat it* (1861), talks of a life out of water of well over a week and even longer if you make up a brine of 'sulphate of magnesia, sulphate of lime, sodium chloride, chloride of magnesia, chloride of potassium, bromide of magnesium and carbonate of lime'. Ostend oysters were sent to Moscow, arriving fresh and lively after seventeen days in a covered basket. [1981]

QUAIL

Quail have experienced a revival. Once, they were shot wild or netted here while on their summer visits. Migratory in habit, they winter in northern Africa and were netted in myriads as they traversed the Mediterranean. The inhuman practice (outlawed in England in 1937 as, too, is shooting them today) was the subject of a letter in 1914 from the naturalist W. H. Hudson to Norman Douglas (quoted in the latter's spasmodic memoirs, *Looking Back*, 1932). Therein, writing in praise of a piece by Douglas, Hudson refers on the one hand to Italian and Greek islanders blinding decoy quails before setting them out as lures to the migrants and on the other to the source of many quails for British tables: Egypt.

I daresay you know all about the Italian share in the detestable business, but I doubt that you have full knowledge of the whole thing: we know it was reported that the Greeks blind the birds at Cerigo and other islands where quails are [one word illegible] in great numbers; but it has not been established that they do so. Nor can the young be left to starve when the birds are caught on the spring migration. Another thing: I fancy if you had known all the facts you would have put in a word about England's refusal to cooperate with Germany and France in 1897 when it was proposed that the three countries should forbid the importation of quails during the close season for other game birds. Our government declined and as we are the biggest consumers nothing could be done. The result is that the quail is vanishing from a great part of Europe as it has vanished from this country ... In 1904 the Bird Protection Society made an appeal to Lord Cromer [Consul-General of Egypt] on the subject and there was a decree made prohibiting the [?capture] of quails at less distance than 1000 metres from the coast. It is on the coast that they are netted in vast numbers ... when they congregate before taking their flight over the seas.

As with most such luxuries, the trade took a beating with the upsets of our world in the thirties and the forties. Out of recession was born the trade of farming quails for the table and it is from such farms that the new hedonists are supplied. Again following a pattern, the farmed commodity needs very careful handling if it is to taste of anything. One of the first such farms in England was in Devon: Willestrew Quail, founded near Tavistock by Mr Owen Moreshead. By 1980 there were some thirteen major quail producers throughout the country. This number has subsequently increased. It was to Willestrew that we first repaired for supplies of fresh birds. It was from K. J. Callender, the then owner, that I gained the following facts.

The quail are Japanese, the variety or strain Courtenay. The farm kills between 1,000 and 1,500 per week and sells about 150 dozen eggs. The flock is 10,000 strong, of which 1,000 are breeding. The latter group is made up of three females to each male. Each hen lays about five eggs a week which are either sold as eggs or hatched in an incubator. There is a low fertility rate of about 55 per cent but mortality is not bad. Of 1,200 chicks, only about 100 are lost by the time they reach six weeks. The birds are fed a high-protein turkey meal. The adults live at a constant 70°F, the chicks at 101°F. Power cuts can deal a death blow to whole flocks.

Willestrew quail are about five ounces dressed weight. This is larger than the French birds (about three and a half ounces) and many from England. This is partly because Mr Callender kills at over six weeks, as opposed to the norm of five; it is also because the Willestrew flock is genetically strong. A great deal of trouble should be taken in selecting and maintaining the right strain. Another variety, the American Bobwhite, can be found in this country. It is a larger bird, but more sensitive to variation in temperature.

Of the average weekly production of 1,000 at least half will be boned out before dispatch and the vast majority are frozen. Only two of his customers – ourselves and another restaurant – take them 'long legged': with the legs still on, the gut intact and unfrozen. We feel that this is the only way to buy them. If they are processed as soon as they are killed, their flavour is nonexistent. If allowed to mature for a few days with the gut in, the flavour improves. Our normal practice is to roast them with the gut still in, though it should be noted that if the birds are mature and egg laying, you are likely to have an egg in the gut which pops out during the cooking – a disconcerting thing to have on the plate. The trail is not something of a delicacy in the way of woodcock, so it is no loss to rid the bird of its innards before serving.

Boning the birds is a tedious process, undertaken by the farm only to ensure that customers keep returning. Plucking, using a machine, is easier. They dip in hot water before putting through the machine and then hand finishing. As may be imagined, labour is female and part time. Transport and delivery is the bugbear of small businesses in extended districts like South Devon. We had some close shaves with missing the train from Plymouth or the 'bus connection through Kingsbridge. You can trace the parcel by the smell.

Maturing poultry with the gut in is a subject to which we revert at various times throughout this book. The disappearance of this practice, together with the inveterate use of frozen birds, is the chief cause for quail having such a lowly reputation. If you combine these factors with the total lack of exercise that reared birds have had by contrast to their migratory forebears, it is evident that they will have little resemblance to the taste of earlier times. Nonetheless, they can be a toothsome morsel.

The quail is a prolific layer. Its egg has thus become a favourite toy of chefs the world over, especially with the demise of other more recondite sorts. For my taste, it is a little sweet when cooked without trimmings, but the flavour is very delicate. The most famous dish has to be the small boats of quail eggs with a duxelles and a *hollandaise* elaborated at the Connaught Hotel, but a luxurious and simple beginning can be made by baking the eggs with a little cream and tarragon.

THE SERVICE CHARGE IN RESTAURANTS

When we opened at Dartmouth in 1974 we had a note on the bottom of the menu that read, 'The prices include VAT and service and there is no need to add any further tip'. In later years this was shortened to 'Prices are inclusive of VAT and service', then to 'Prices are inclusive' with a further note on each bill: 'Totally inclusive'. When the client read the first phrase, he assumed that we levied a covert 12 per cent and distributed it to the staff. This was inaccurate, so we changed to the last development which was to make a small folder for the bill, detailing credit cards, foreign exchange regulations and including a note that staff and management neither expected nor demanded tips.

Wages earned by staff should be fixed at a mutually acceptable level and should not vary according to season or the good-will of the customer. We would return tips given without an understanding of this principle. Paying for a meal in a restaurant should be a commercial transaction no different in kind from purchasing shoes or groceries. The several levels of payment customarily exacted from clients are obnoxious, whether taken as of right by a management that adds a service charge to the bill or extracted by notes on the menus and invoices that prices do *not* include service. There is a prissiness about money in hotels and restaurants that is distasteful. Equally, we have ever deplored the customer who demands his right to tip so as to maintain some form of advantage over the staff.

For years, the industry has agonised about inclusive charges. Mostly, this has centred on VAT. That anyone can be as obtuse as restaurant managers have shown themselves to be is quite devastating. That a hotel chain can charge £10, then add 15 per cent service and VAT at 8 per cent, as Trust House Forte used to do in the old days, yet remain surprised when someone objected to this as a monstrous ramp is difficult to comprehend. Yet the same nonsense about business users (who do not worry about VAT, as it is deductible), or about a government imposition unconnected with the true charge they are making (it is an imposition, I agree, but no different in kind from income tax) is trotted out by every section of the industry. At last, Parliament has tried to deal with these matters but, even so, there are people who avoid the spirit while abiding by the letter of the law. When the first regulations were made governing the display of prices at the entrance to any restaurant, it was compulsory that they show VAT in the figures given. Nonetheless there were many establishments that performed this part of the law but retained old-style menus indoors – hence the need for more rigorous ministerial intervention. The Restaurateurs' Association of Great Britain attempts to justify independence with statements like, 'The attitude of the Minister is to treat customers as idiots, but they are not. If you go into an establishment which does not say prices include VAT then the customer knows that VAT will be added to the bill'. True, but adding a service charge *and* VAT at 15 per cent, puts another 30 per cent on the total and, no matter how canny we are, we do not keep a running total of the meal in our heads as we munch our way through.

Discussion of VAT hardly touches on tips, save that the ambivalence extends to them too. Recognition that they exist spreads from top to bottom of the system. Even the Catering Wages Council allows a lower minimum wage to workers who are in contact with the tipping public, on the grounds that their wages will be made up from gratuities. To rid ourselves of this detestable hangover of servility and sharp practice will take a long time.

The existence of a service charge, added in the form of a percentage on the bill, has always raised interesting questions. Take a small but world-famous hotel in the Highlands with a turnover, judging from profiles, somewhere in the region of £500,000 with a service charge of 12½ per cent. If the hotel pays its staff the minimum laid down by the Wages Council and then distributes its percentage between a personnel of 40, then the staff is by no means badly paid: certainly better than on a production line. Yet we are told that our industry is poorly paid and exploitative. Perhaps some places, rather than distributing the charge, swallow it and use it to pay the wages. Perhaps the charge is another way of increasing the bill to the customer, for there is no legal compulsion to share it between the staff, any more than there is a need to spend the money raised by the cover charge on new linen and cutlery, or the road tax on road improvements.

Servitude is the destroyer of the social fabric and it is long since Britain was a wholly servile nation. In 1841, in Dartmouth, a town not filled with aristocrats or the well-to-do, 22 per cent of the employed population was in service. Yet readings of any realist novelist of the eighteenth and nineteenth centuries, Smollett or Surtees for example, will show how unsatisfactory was the master/servant relation, how it was open to abuse from both sides. An author such as Surtees would underline that the faults were as often the employers' as the employees'. The class as a whole was ripe for revolt though an opportunity was not found until the two world wars. The catering industry is the last outpost of the servant class and we are still living with the effects of that revolt. Its members are still smarting under the yoke of servitude and, after witnessing customers treat workers in much the same way as South Africans speak to Kaffirs, I am not surprised there is some truculence and unwillingness. There is still a mutual resentment that some societies, republics like France and the United States, may have gone further (though not all the way) in escaping.

It is because the customer has down-graded the social standing of waiters that foreign immigrants had the chance to take over most of the service tasks in hotels. In Europe there has never been the social stigma attached to cooking and practical support roles – save that of kitchen porter, reserved for the foundations of the social pyramid. Foreign workers, because they do not form part of the social system, can afford to ignore the nuances of hierarchical behaviour displayed by their clients and have the advantage of their nationality to protect their identities. Who can forget the late banqueting manager of the Savoy, a Welshman who worked all his days under an assumed Italian name so as to preserve the preconceptions of his customers?

There is a confrontational element to the waiter/client relationship at the root of many of the difficulties experienced by English service staff. The customer is convinced, perhaps on secular precedent, that he will be duped; the waiter knows he must preserve the initiative if he is not to be exploited. The customer has simple ruses in his battery: discovering the first name of the staff, demanding attention at every turn, making him wait for his order, presuming the worst about the cooking or the wine, using the expectation of a tip as a sword of Damocles. The waiter's parries include ignorance, presumption of superior knowledge, adoption of foreign accents, preoccupation elsewhere, an insufferable *hauteur*. Hostilities need never break out; most moves are retaliatory. Similar patterns may be encountered in France and Italy at only the most expensive houses. Arrogance and insolence go together where the identity of the staff is threatened by the insouciant aggression of the customer. Unfortunately, the response becomes habitual and the worst manifestations are often visited upon the most blameless and meekest of couples living it up for a night; never to repeat the experience.

The English class system is enshrined within the linguistic patterns of its participants in a way shared by no other culture. A sociological study, *The World of Waiters* (Mars and Nicod, 1984), writes, 'Waiters address a customer by his or her surname, or as "Sir" or "Madam". Obviously, these forms of address demonstrate the deference of those serving . . .' The undertones of 'deference' are neither courtesy nor recognition of the factual relationship between client and waiter. A refusal to accept these forms of address is sometimes encountered in Americans who feel them too redolent of an old order. However, the Revolution in France allowed them to spread through the social fabric, assuaging the most prickly of egalitarians. A similarly levelling usage is found in England when the police address a citizen: there is no doubt to whom the initiative belongs, yet the expression of respect persists.

We endorse hierarchies to an extent unparalleled by other western groups: who else would permit such a royal family? Yet we preserve a curmudgeonly individualism that will have no truck with personal service. The way out of the impasse is to invest the function of service with self-respect. There are signs that this may still occur, without wholesale abdication to immigrant control. A pre-requisite is that tipping stops. It encapsulates the whole dirty business – not a financial transaction, an expression of social control. Together with many other service industries, catering has attracted greater status as the bourgeoisie itself takes on the role of restaurateur, country house hotelier or chef. The same process is perceptible with waiting. Though chefs and managers retain the greatest cachet, the employment of middle-class girls has leavened the expression of social aggression in the dining room. True, they have not spread to the more professional areas of the industry, still the preserve of the foreigner, but they have altered the face of English country dining. Signs of the craft of waiting being treated with the seriousness of that of cooking by the educational institutions are few, even if basic training is allowed. This is the next step; one taken already by a few of the more enlightened bodies connected with the industry.

December

DECEMBER DIARY

The month has brought its play of showers upon the parched breast of Devon. Springs rise where none was known before. The pond at Allaleigh, empty when last I wrote, is now overflowing. The ducks, at least, are happy. Markets did not occur on the quays of Brixham during the worst of the gales; and they were weak elsewhere. Prices for fish were accordingly high. [1984]

This can be a dreadful month. Shops in Dartmouth present the same lugubrious show of winter crops lightened by nuts, oranges, lemons and apples. At least, it seems like that on bad days. With a stir of optimism and a dash of hope, all is not quite so black. The more enterprising are importing fennel, mangoes, kiwi, ogens, mange-touts and French beans. Marks and Spencer have excellent broccoli from Spain and have just started the new season's clementines; the autumn and winter crops are at their peak: carrots, celery, leeks, celeriac, beetroots, cauliflower and calabrese, even if not *en primeur* do taste pretty good and are in fine condition. [1981]

Dandelions that have been planted for us are beginning their blanching, they will be ready for the new year. Landcress which I had sown in October is being picked. The watercress has not been very exciting recently so the fresh hot taste of landcress seedlings was welcome. [1981]

The best thing in the vegetable markets has been Italian new potatoes, packed in sand. Their breed is indeterminate, but they are of yellow flesh, have been well dug and treated, are still scraping and have as good a taste as many of the English product offered by merchants in high summer. They are vastly superior to the Canary, Jersey or Egyptian tubers. They are also cheaper. [1982]

The best fruit this year has been Conference pears grown by Mr Peter

Barry Mehew in the Delicatessen, Dartmouth.

Wheldon at Newton Leys in Suffolk. Of perfect size and condition, with an intense flavour, they have been used as an accompaniment to venison, after being poached in red wine. The venison has been supplied by Heal Farm in north Devon from a herd in Petworth, Sussex. The animals are fallow deer, called prickets, i.e. in their second year, with straight horns. We have taken loins alone. The meat is tender, though not excessively so, and the flavour relatively light. [1982]

Poultry has been making its Christmas impact. We have had some excellent geese from Mrs Jane Reeves of Higher Barn Farm near Dartmouth. Earlier supplies from her yard included Indian Game chicken and Khaki Campbell ducks. They have been cut short by the depredations of the fox. We are trying a terrine of goose and chicken livers in the manner of a *terrine de foie gras frais* because we have had so many goose livers and Mrs Shillabeer's chicken livers have been so large and pale, with a mild flavour. The result cannot be compared to its Landais original, but nor should it be. However, it was an interesting dish that showed that really good livers are worth treating on their own even if we do not go to the lengths of fattening of the French. [1981]

Guinea fowl have continued in small numbers. We have marinated them with basil, parsley, lemon and oil, split them in half and grilled them, serving with either a paprika and cream cheese sauce or a watercress sauce. Game has also been making regular appearance. The pheasants have been good, as have ducks. There have been a few woodcock and snipe; the cold weather will doubtless bring more woodcock. I was being told the other day that we should be encouraging our shooters to pour Calvados down the throat of a woodcock immediately after it has been retrieved so that the trail can be made still more delicious! [1981]

Game has come in steadily although with little variety. Too early, so far, for woodcock. We had a wild duck that had been ringed by the Irish Forest and Wildlife Service. I sent the ring back to see its life history. The reply was an object lesson in our inability to recognise biological facts. The bird was ringed in August 1981 in County Wexford and shot at Slapton fifteen months later. It was four years old. Its breast was still quite tender. [1982]

The port of Dartmouth is profiting for the first time from the upsurge in mackerel fishing in the south west. The river has become the winter home of two Bulgarian factory ships, grading horse mackerel or scad. These are sold by the eastern bloc to Africa. It has not been explained why we do not exploit the riches of our own seas for ourselves. There is also a Norwegian ship accepting catches of sprats. The town is suddenly full of Slav sailors clutching shoes or toys to their chests. [1981]

Fishing off Cornwall this autumn has shown new trends. The Looe fleet of long-liners (who go after mackerel especially) have complained of a poor season. In part the cause is the markets. They have to sell at Plymouth, thus pay fees twice, at Looe and at the market itself. They have also found that their catch is sold at the end of the auction session, after the Plymouth boats, thus reaching less satisfactory prices. Alternatives to mackerel fishing, especially monkfish and squid, have not yet been successful. Looe trawlers had equipped themselves with squid jigging gear, embarking in the last few years on a whole new sort of fishery, more redolent of the Mediterranean than northern seas. However, the fish have not been there for the catching. [1984]

New facts about cider come up every month. The latest is confirmation that Devonshire and cider producers' tastes have differed from those of their customers. The Rev. Thomas Moore observed in 1829 that 'the cider in general use is that which has undergone the vinous fermentation, and has consequently become strong and hard, which, though it agrees with the natives, seems much too acid to strangers, and in them causes flatulence and the colic, frequently to a serious and alarming degree. The sweet cider is obtained, not from different fruit, but by checking fermentation by repeatedly racking it off, preparing the casks by burning brimstone in them, and other arts. This is prepared for the metropolis, and for general exportation; but it does not suit the taste of the inhabitants of Devonshire, nor, as it is said, does it afford the nourishment and strength which it yields when it is properly fermented.' [1982]

JOHN GLASSBROOK — FISHMONGER

It may be understood that, for a restaurant by the seaside, the supply of fish was of prime importance. Our relations with John Glassbrook, fishmonger *extraordinaire* of Dartmouth, occupied much time, care and pleasure. His retirement in 1983 was a benchmark in our own development. One signal characteristic was his extensive background in fishmongering, both as a retailer and a processor or producer. We could rely upon him not only to supply good material, but to have information about its wider significance and a perspective on its role in the fish trade of earlier years. His training and contacts from a life in the Home Counties meant that he could engineer supplies of London goods that we would have otherwise found unobtainable. His experience of poultry and fish meant that few things came through our door about which he was not more knowledgeable than ourselves, even if his activities did not stretch as far as the stove top.

He was born just after the First World War, above a fishmonger's shop. His parents had shops in Englefield Green, in the parish of Egham, and in Sunningdale. Royal Ascot and the large houses that peppered this district, and continued to be built throughout the twenties and thirties, bulked large in the economic calculations of the family business. He started work for his father when fourteen, as a delivery boy. Learning the ropes in this way for three years, he then went as a poulterer at Sainsbury's in 1938. This, however, was not to last many months before call-up to the Militia in the wake of the Munich Crisis. The outbreak of war saw Mr Glassbrook in the 51st Highland Division. Hostilities were short and sharp; he was taken prisoner of war at St Valéry in the aftermath of Dunkirk and remained in eastern Germany and Poland until liberation and demobilisation. Returning to Surrey, he took over the running of the business, his parents having indicated a desire to retire. Wish and act do not necessarily synchronise and the transfer to the next generation evidently took some years. The end result was that John Glassbrook had the Englefield Green branch and his brother took on Sunningdale. John added a fried fish shop to his enterprise, leaving it under management but supplying it through the main business.

Matters might have remained like this had not one of his customers been involved in acquiring control of Porthleven Harbour in Cornwall. Porthleven, situated mid-way between Land's End and the Lizard, was a small fishing settlement that had been developed after the Napoleonic Wars, the harbour constructed to profit from the copper and tin production of the district. It was never very successful; a certain trade exporting ores and metals and china clay and china stone; small reciprocal imports of coal, agricultural goods, lime and building materials. The last commercial vessel emptied its holds in 1958. The port was more useful as a crabbing and inshore trawling centre. The new owners, at the end of the fifties, found themselves with a small fleet of crab-boats of their own and income from landings on their quays of other crabbers. They asked John to report on how best to utilise this business. His recommendation was to construct live tanks for lobsters and crayfish and erect a processing factory for crabmeat. The tanks enabled the prime fish to be held for export to France and Spain. Lobsters were packed and air freighted to France, many of the crayfish sent by sea to Spain, the ships with well-holds taking in salt water so the cargo would not deteriorate. The crabs were picked on the spot providing both local employment and control of the marketing of the crabmeat. Where fishermen trunk their catch of live crabs to Billingsgate, packed in tea chests, there is ever a danger of spoilage and mortality. It may happen that death is claimed where none occurred, to the loss of the fisherman, not the wholesaler or carrier. Thus many boats would rather sell locally, be it to the immediate consumer or to a processor. They are assured payment for the whole of their product. This has happened increasingly on the Kingswear quay; very few boats now send to London. Mr Glassbrook's scheme proposed a similar solution for Porthleven. The white meat would be sold to frozen food firms, or for the fresh picked market; the brown meat would go to the fishpaste manufacturers; the shells would be collected each day and ground for fertiliser and bone meal. John recalls justification for this policy. A telephone call from London asked for a large shipment of crabs, at any price, the next morning. He responded by hiring a five-tonner and driving it up himself. Greeted at the market with jubilation, he was urged to take breakfast while the lorry was unloaded. Sure that on his return he would find that half had been condemned and spirited out of sight, he stuck to his post until the ticket had been signed. As he says, 'Did he clean up that day.'

This venture, developing from a report into a full-scale implementation and management post, occupied Mr Glassbrook for five years. In the interim, he sold his businesses in Englefield Green and settled properly in Cornwall. Although Porthleven got off to a good start, the commercial histories of the firms that had control of the harbour were not encouraging. Each in turn was taken over or went broke and the factory and tanks are now derelict. The centre for west Cornish shellfishing moved firmly to Newlyn. John was not in Porthleven to witness this decline. After leaving the quays, he lived on the Lizard peninsular for a year or two, for once in his life having nothing to do with the fishing industry. Then he returned, for family reasons, to the Home Counties, starting a small fishmonger's in part of a butcher's shop in Sandhurst, Camberley. His experience of the area served him well, but he had developed a taste for the south-west that re-surfaced when there was no longer reason to stay near London. This occurred in 1970/71 when he came to Dartmouth and bought Fleet's, a long established fish and game dealer in Foss Street. It was there that we met him.

There were two fish shops in the town, plus a market stall on Fridays. Fleet's had the select business as well as most of the trade accounts. Glassbrook's immediate predecessors were two energetic men who had perhaps revived a moribund business, engaging in adventurous buying and creative marketing. They went over the river to start the popular John Dory restaurant in Torquay, specialising in fish and game. Retail business at Fleet's continued for ten years when the Glassbrooks decided that the bulk of trade was with hotels and restaurants and they could be as well served out of a small industrial unit as a shop. The Foss Street premises was therefore sold, without the goodwill, and he moved to a small warehouse on Jawbones, overlooking Dartmouth from the water tower and the site of the former town abattoir and isolation hospital (separate but contiguous buildings!). He continued in this guise, taking orders by telephone, going to market and delivering out of Jawbones, until 1983 when he sold as a going concern in order to retire. His successors were able to buy the second fish retailer in the town and now combine the two sorts of trade, together with a wholesale fish trunking business working out of Brixham market.

His first job paid five shillings a week, at the age of fourteen, as a delivery bike boy; each day from eight in the morning until the rounds were finished; on Sunday, a morning delivery. The Englefield Green shop had five lads, as well as two ponies and traps, replaced first by a motor cycle combination, then a bullnose Morris. The bicycles had large wheels front and back. The small front-wheeled trade bike was not adopted until the mid-thirties. Imagine, then, the height of the centre of gravity of a large wheeled cycle with a fully laden metal basket high above the front brake. Deliveries were the life-blood of the business. Cash trade was minimal; lucky if they took fifteen shillings in the day. Yet a full display was created on the slab each morning, cooled by a block of ice at its summit. The routine was an early morning round to drop the breakfast kippers and late orders for luncheon, in the course of which requests for deliveries later in the day would be received. These relayed to base, an order was placed on the telephone with the Billingsgate agent (the bummaree) by midday and would be on the station platform by 3.30. An earlier delivery, prompted by a five o'clock call, would have been left at the station by 8.30 in the morning.

Bummaree is a word first noticed in 1786; its origins are obscure. It may be related to the earlier term, bottomry, which related to the practice of a master borrowing money for a voyage on the security of a ship itself. The element of trust and expenditure on another's behalf implicit in the Billingsgate relationship may have given rise to this linguistic analogy. The bummaree worked on commission. The speed of transmission that came from the rail network in the late nineteenth century is always remarkable. The fish trains that set off each day from the main ports to Billingsgate and to other urban centres were a regular feature until the very recent past. However, a word of caution from Aflalo (*The Sea-fishing Industry of England and Wales*, 1904) on the breakdown of the chain when cargo was discharged from trains to horse vans in the streets of London: congestion was so bad at Billingsgate itself that the vans might wait from six to eight hours before unloading. The twice daily delivery did not last through the war. As staff became harder to find and the telephone more widely spread, the early morning drop could be cut out. Replacement of bicycles by motor transport also helped in this respect.

The perfect medium for keeping fish is ice. Refrigeration dries it out. Proper icing keeps it at the right temperature and in the right conditions. Of course, it is not an indefinite solution and the Glassbrook enterprise was fortunate in its reliance on a low casual element in its trade. Very little was bought except on order. There was thus small carry-over from day to day. The fish was kept in one-inch slate-slab boxes, layered with ice. Even in the 1970s, John Glassbrook only put his day's purchase into the fridge at the end of the afternoon. Until then it was in trays under ice in the work room. Ice came from the refrigeration plant at Kingston upon Thames; up to two tons each day during the summer, when they would have two deliveries. It came in hundredweight blocks, broken up at the shop with picks and needles. The fishmonger was the source of ice for every house's ice-box and great blocks would have to be delivered on the front of the bike by the intrepid boys. John recalls taking one to the royal lodge in Windsor Park and coming to an emergency halt in the drive, obstructed by a Personage's perambulator. The bike may have stopped but the ice did not, describing a graceful arc over the carriage. How near we court notoriety. To keep the ice from one day to the next delivery, there was a great well in the back yard, the neighbour of the sawdust store for the floor. A singularly unfortunate improver once mistook breadcrumbs for sawdust – a start to a crunchy day at the shop. The presence of ice led to the development of ice cream as part of the fishmonger's stock in trade. The Glassbrooks were the first in the district to take Wall's product, keeping it in wooden boxes packed with ice and salt. In this manner, it would last perhaps a week. When we first came to Dartmouth, John was still pursuing this line, although with a freezer. He was the only stockist of Bertorelli for miles around.

In the early thirties, the Englefield Green shop had three men on the fish block, two poulterers and five delivery boys, as well as John's mother supervising the cash and accounts. This level of staff could not survive the war. Trade was much reduced, fish was on quota, staff were difficult to train or find. The establishment was reduced to two men on the block, a part-timer and John doing the deliveries. They were perhaps helped, as easier times came along, by the intensive residential developments of that district: the Wentworth estate and golf course for one. The character of that is epitomised in Agatha Christie's description of 'Styles', the house she and her husband renamed when they moved there in 1926, 'a sort of millionaire-style Savoy suite transferred to the country ... quantities of bathrooms, basins in bedrooms and everything.' For the Glassbrooks, the density of millionaires, resident cooks and staff as well as spendthrift Ascot visitors was just the ticket. John recalls how these temporary establishments for Royal Ascot might be set up. A cook would be got out of retirement, a formidable cook, who knew what she wanted and needed immediate service for the duration of her stint, who would brook no gainsaying, but who would pay for it: a bankroll on the kitchen table as a sweetener to the initial negotiations. And then, no stopping them: parties, guests, the best, the extravagant. To a boy on five shillings weekly, the chance of tips, food and drink to be garnered from an evening spent manning an oyster bar opening the shells for assembled party-goers was a prospect of Xanadu. Lesser earnings might be made from delivering oysters for a dinner party at a pre-appointed time and opening them in the kitchen. This was standard practice.

The level of preparation and finish was greater than it is today.

Smoked salmon was always sliced; oysters always opened; whiting skinned and curled. Now, we count ourselves lucky to get the fish itself. In no area is this revealed better than poultry and game. It will have been noted that there were two poulterers to three fishmongers on the staff of the shop. Evidently, the skills were interchangeable in a rush, but the ratio broadly reflected trade. Many birds and game came from Leadenhall until that market shifted towards oven-ready and retail business and Smithfield became the main source. However, at Chertsey, the family had its own poultry farm, raising hens, chickens, capons and ducks. Turkeys were avoided because of their susceptibility to disease. Some game would come from local shoots and they had the marketing for the entire product of some syndicates so the traffic with Smithfield would be two-way. Rabbits, too, would be bought locally – only snared or netted, never shot. Sometimes these were bought from trappers who worked far afield, displaying their catch on long poles racked in the back of a van. The shop would take the whole yield from the clearance of Windsor Great Park, an annual affair. This would be so large that the meat could not be kept as long as its consumption would demand. Thus the entire workforce would settle down to skinning; the bodies were buried on the allotment and the pelts rubbed in sawdust and stretched on wires, awaiting purchase by the fur merchant.

The allotment was evidently a rich and fertile spot. It took the leavings of many processes. Aflalo, already mentioned, observed that the price received for rotting fish from the manure industry declined as artificial substances had been invented. The pet-food business was in its infancy, even if pig-swill was still permitted. One is reminded of Dallas's entry in *Kettner's Book of the Table* (1877) under sprats: 'Sprats and their euthanasia. The following receipt for turning sprats into roses – the sublime of cookery – is borrowed from a private letter: – "Some time since C— went to visit a friend in the country who had the most marvellous roses in full bloom. Every one exclaimed at their beauty and asked, 'How can you get such?' The gentleman who owned them was a man of few words, and only said – 'Sprats.' It seems he manured them with loads of stinking sprats. Not long afterwards a man called at my house with sprats. 'Are they stinking?' said I, eagerly. 'No,' said the man – 'quite fresh.' 'Then bring me the first stinking ones you have.' In a few days he came with a heavy heart, and offered me a large quantity which had turned putrid on his hands. The result was that on a very small bush I had thirty-six blossoms all at once of magnificent Marshal Niels."'

The scale of importation of poultry was quite as large as it is today:

quail from Egypt, pigeons from France, guinea fowl from Poland. All had to be dressed and trussed in the shop, even, in the case of pigeons, prepared for cooking with a *foie gras* stuffing. Hares too would be prepared for jugging, cut into pieces, or trussed for roasting, with the head standing erect, ears outstretched just as in a Beeton engraving. Such elaboration has gone, except from the most old fashioned or expensive outlets, though retailers, even the largest of them, are perhaps finding now that customers are wooed to novelties with a degree of presentation. However, the structure of trade has changed, with emphasis on finishing having passed to the processors and packagers rather than the front-line retailers.

John Glassbrook is a council member of the National Fishmongers' Federation. He, then, should have a view on the relative decline of the trade over past decades. To him, the major onslaught came with the reappraisal of high street sites which caused greater burdens of rents, rates and other fixed overheads. Their effect, when combined with competition from other forms of food retailing and new interpretations of fish as a foodstuff – scampi and frozen fish fingers – was to diminish the number of retail outlets. An ageing labour force, with little new blood, was a complicating factor. Conditions of work: early hours, cold hands, wet feet, high smell, moderate wages, have ever been hard by contrast to many. Yet the job is bound to be labour intensive and more difficult to mechanise or streamline in the way of some tasks in meat butchery. It is probably this relation of labour and fixed overheads to turnover that has been the bedevilling factor in the trade for there is little way out of it: a fish superstore is not the answer. There have been some recent improvements: government bodies and the Federation have smartened up the image of the trade; the number of retailers is again on the increase. The greater balance that John Glassbrook would like to see struck is that between meat prices and fish prices. Were the former to be set at a true level, undistorted by subsidy, perhaps national intake of fish would increase still further. Yet, the Elizabethan experiments in extending the numbers of fish days through the week may indicate that tastes need to be changed more radically than by mere market manipulation.

Recipes

Unless otherwise stated, these recipes give four servings

Carved Angel
DARTMOUTH
Devon

2 South
Embankment
Dartmouth
2465

Closed Jan;
Boxing Day;
Mon; Sun D
Must book D
Meals 12.30–
2.30, 6.30–11

Alc £4.05 (meal
£5.30)

VAT & service
inc
Children's
helpings
Seats 40 (Parties
15)
&. rest (3 steps)
No dogs

Entry in *Good
Food Guide*,
1976

We needs must love the highest when we see it, and visitors offer thanksgivings for this quayside restaurant designed and run by Tom Jaine, George Perry-Smith's stepson, with Joyce Molyneux in the kitchen, as at the Bath Hole in the Wall of old. At the end of a meal totally without sin, reports a visiting parson, 'the chocolate and almond meringue cake (two helpings offered and greedily consumed) was clearly a carved angel of light masquerading as a demon, Gluttony, and causing a poor vicar to stumble. Thank goodness that my stipend goes up soon.' A peer of the realm evidently had similar feelings: far from being bothered by a sense of exposure behind the huge window that looks out of the harbour and the multicoloured sails, 'like early Christians we longed for those outside to come in'. Those who venture go upstairs now to a lounge where they may drink, nibble the very best and plumpest of black olives, and browse through Mr Jaine's books or look at his Edward Lear topographical prints. Avoid Saturday nights if possible. One quiet August lunchtime an inspector just returned from France had a meal of a quality and equipoise hard to find on either side of the Channel: the lightest of gnocchi with a home-made pesto (75p), aïoli garni (£2.60), with turbot, lightly cooked green vegetables, potatoes, and as a visual master stroke, yellow tomatoes, and peaches in brandy and lemon, with the lemon slices as compellingly edible as the peaches. The fish soups, the eggs with tapénade, the 'innocent and excellent' sea bass with mayonnaise verte, the spiced chicken croquettes with Joyce's remarkable lemon pickle, the moussaka, the grey mullet stuffed with lemon and herbs, served with a prawn sauce, the freshly fried aubergines, an Easter cake at Easter and a summer pudding in summer: all these and many more set a standard of conception and, almost invariably, of achievement that should be studied even where it cannot be imitated. The wines, though not yet the service of them, are worthy of the food and, in the lower reaches, modestly priced. You will not be drinking Ch. Capbern '37, c.b., at £18 every day, but it was a lucky inspector who ordered Côtes du Rhône white and found himself drinking Yapp's 'Cépage Viognier' from a Condrieu grower at only £2.90. Note that VAT and service are included in prices. No music. The carved angel's belly is splitting: no wonder, poor girl.

App: by too many members to list

Soups

BANANA CURRY SOUP

A way to use those bananas when they go too far in the fruit bowl, or bought cheaply from the greengrocer at the end of the week.

6oz / 160g onion
2oz / 50g butter
2 teaspoons flour
2 teaspoons curry powder
1lb / 450g ripe bananas

1fl oz / 30ml lemon juice
1fl oz / 30ml water
2 pints / 1.2l chicken stock
3fl oz / 90ml double cream

Sweat very finely chopped onion in butter. When they are softened, add the flour and curry powder and fry some more. Skin the bananas and cut them into a blender with the lemon juice and water. Blend to a purée and add to the onions. Add the stock. Bring to the boil, season and simmer for fifteen minutes. Add double cream to taste.

LETTUCE AND MINT SOUP

1 onion
2oz / 50g butter
1 lettuce
1½ pints / 900ml ham stock

3 sprigs mint
5fl oz / 120ml double cream
Salt, pepper, sugar

Peel and chop the onion, sweat it in butter. Shred the lettuce and add that to the onion; continue to sweat. Add the water from cooking a ham. It should not be too strong, so check for salt. Simmer for five minutes. Add the mint. Put through the blender and the fine plate of the food mill. Bring back to the boil on the stove and finish with cream. Check for seasoning; the lettuce may need a little sugar. If it is very strong-tasting lettuce, it may need prior blanching and refreshing.

A summer soup does not need much thickening. However, a *liaison* of egg yolks may be made with the cream, and the soup not boiled afterwards.

CARROT AND CORIANDER SOUP

A good winter soup, better for clamped rather than bunch carrots.

4oz / 100g onions
1lb / 450g carrots
2oz / 50g butter
1 dessertspoon coriander,
    ground finely

2 pints / 1.2l chicken stock
Double cream
Salt and pepper

Peel and slice the onion and carrot. Sweat them in the butter in a covered pan for twenty minutes. Add the ground coriander. Add the stock and the seasoning. Simmer gently for fifteen minutes. Blend until smooth or put through the fine plate of a food mill. Put back on the heat and finish with cream. Check for seasoning.

PEAR AND WATERCRESS SOUP

That none of us is immune from fashion is a truism. This recipe, for that most fashionable of fruits, is witness. It comes from Jeremiah Tower, of San Francisco, and was printed in the first issue of *Petits Propos Culinaires*, and then in the *Time-Life* book of soups. I think his original idea was for a cold soup, whereas we serve it hot. There are fewer pears in the version we cook now, so that it does not taste so fruited. Mr Tower counselled a generous seasoning with lemon juice to avoid excess sweetness. This is not so necessary.

1½lbs / 675g pears
4oz / 110g watercress
2 pt / 1.2l chicken stock

Salt, pepper and lemon juice
5fl oz / 150ml double cream

Peel, quarter and core the pears. Wash the watercress. Put the debris of the pears with half the stock and boil. Blanch the quarters with the other half. Strain the stock off the debris and put it with the pears and rest of the stock in a liquidiser. Add the watercress. Blend well. Finish through the fine plate of a food mill or a medium sieve. Watercress soups are too stringy to avoid this last process. Season and finish with cream.

There is no need to blanch the watercress before adding it to the blender of hot stock.

Cold beginnings

AN AUBERGINE, COCONUT AND CUMIN CUSTARD

An interesting first course can be made by offering three dishes of aubergine – a 'caviar', an *imam bayildi* and this custard. The recipes for the first two can be found in books by Jane Grigson, Claudia Roden, Arabella Boxer and Elizabeth David. This custard began life as a recipe by Alice Wooledge Salmon in *House and Garden*. There, she suggested a *gratin* of dried coconut, *fromage blanc* and aubergine. Instead, Joyce Molyneux added cumin, reduced the amount of coconut and made a mould that could be eaten as a cool first course.

12oz / 325g aubergine	Pinch of cumin
2 cloves garlic	Salt and pepper
2 eggs	1oz / 25g grated, creamed
8fl oz / 240ml yoghurt or sour	coconut
cream	

Peel and slice the aubergine. Steam it until tender. Chop the garlic finely and cook very gently in a little olive oil. Chop the steamed aubergine and mix it well with the rest of the ingredients. Taste for seasoning. Put the result in a mould (we used a small loaf tin) and place it in a water bath. It will cook in an hour in an ultra-cool oven 130°C / 250°F / gas mark ½. If it is insufficiently cooked, there will be some free liquid which will make it difficult to handle.

When cooled, it can be turned out of the mould and a slice can be laid on the plate with the other aubergine dishes. You need some dry toast or pitta to eat with it.

TWO CHEESE ICE CREAMS AND A GOAT CHEESE DIP

The excellent St Michael book on ice creams by Heather Lambert gave us these recipes which we changed but slightly, principally by substituting a cream cheese for cottage cheese in the Camembert instructions. It is far less outlandish than you might expect, served as a first course with hot dry brown toast and some vegetable *crudités*. The combination of hot and cold is delectable.

Camembert ice cream

8oz / 225g Camembert	Tabasco
4oz / 110g low fat cream cheese	Black pepper
8fl oz / 240ml double cream	

Break the Camembert into pieces and put it into the food processor with the cream cheese. Blend until smooth. Lightly whip the cream and add a few drops of tabasco and some black pepper. Fold in the cheese mixture. Freeze in a mould lined with clingfilm.

If without a food processor, the same effect can be achieved using a sieve or a food mill. You do not have to take the skin off the Camembert unless it is very horrid.

Goat cheese and hazelnut ice cream

2oz / 50g roasted hazelnuts	5fl oz / 150ml double cream
8oz / 225g goat cheese (the log	1 teaspoon lemon juice
or *roulade* shaped cheese)	Black pepper
5fl oz / 150ml single cream	

Sieve the goat cheese. Mix the single and double creams together and add the cheese, lemon juice and pepper. Skin the hazelnuts by rubbing them in a dry cloth after roasting; chop them. Fold them into the mixture. Freeze them in a similar mould to that used for the Camembert.

Both these cheeses freeze very hard, so a time at room temperature makes them edible – something over an hour.

Goat cheese dip

The *Chez Panisse Menu Cookbook* by Alice Waters (1984) suggests another way of using up old goat cheese that is enjoyed by anyone, even those who do not eat it as a matter of course. This is an adaptation of her recipe.

4oz / 110g goat cheese	1 head garlic
4oz / 110g fat cream cheese	Black pepper
2fl oz / 60ml single cream	

Cut the very top off a head of garlic, put a little thyme and olive oil on it and wrap it in foil. Bake in a medium oven (180°C / 350°F / gas mark 4) until tender, for about 30 minutes. When unwrapped, squeeze the cloves into the cheeses and season with black pepper (salt not necessary with imported French cheese, but may be required for less seasoned English produce). Sieve the cheeses and garlic together. Adjust the texture with single cream.

EGGS WITH A WATERCRESS *MOUSSELINE*

A recipe that we contributed to a book by Michael Raffael, *Five Star Cookery* (1982), is a favourite, yet simplicity itself.

The first requirement is for cold, soft-boiled eggs. This may be achieved by placing the eggs in a saucepan, not too large for the number of eggs, covering them with water from the hot tap, bringing them to the boil on a fast gas and keeping them at a boil for three to three and a half minutes. Then plunge them under the cold tap until they are cool. This should get the required consistency of yolk. Peel them carefully, not too long before you are to eat them. If you tap the shell gently all over with a teaspoon and use the handle of the spoon to free the shell and its skin from the egg, you should extract them without fractures.

For the *mousseline*, take a bunch of watercress, remove the coarsest stalks and wash well. Plunge in boiling water and refresh; drain. Put the watercress in the liquidiser with a coffee cup of single cream and blend to a purée. Whip about a quarter pint of double cream, straight from the refrigerator, so that it is fairly thick. Season it generously with salt and pepper. Add the watercress purée and whip again should that be necessary. The *mousseline* should be slightly thicker than coating. Take care not to over-whip or you may be left with butter if the cream has been kept in too warm a place.

Allow two eggs per person, bedding them on a spoonful of *mousseline* before coating them with more of it. The seasoning of the *mousseline* is important because of the blandness of the eggs.

CALF'S LIVER MOUSSE IN A BRIOCHE

The recipe for brioche is that given on page 199. But half the quantity is all that is needed, so the other half could be made into a small loaf. This mousse is substantial – more suitable for a supper party or buffet. Were it required for a dinner party, the best thing would be to reduce the quantities to one third of those given.

1½lb / 675 g calf's liver	2 eggs
3oz / 75g butter	Seasoning
3oz / 75g flour	1 onion, cloves, bayleaf
16fl oz / 480ml milk	

Infuse the milk with an onion stuck with cloves and the bayleaf. Strain. Make a *roux* with the butter, flour and milk. Leave it to cool. Put the liver, skinned, into a food processor and make a purée. The alternative is to put it through a food mill. Mix the liver with the eggs, the *roux* and some seasoning. Blend again and rub through a fine sieve.

The brioche dough must, of course, be ready; that is, it should have finished its second rise (overnight in a cool room). A raised pie mould suitable for making *pâtés en croûte*, which has hinged sides and a detachable bottom, is very useful. Line this with the brioche dough, pressing it well down into the corners and allowing it to hang over the edges. Roll out a piece of dough to the right size for a lid. Fill the lined mould with the calf's liver mousse, put the lid on and pinch the edges together with the fingers. Leave this to prove for about half an hour. The *mousseline* being raw, it is better not left to hang around for too long.

Bake in a hot oven (240°C / 475°F / gas mark 9) for half an hour. Test its being cooked with an inserted knife. The liver should be pink but not running with blood. It can be served cold or warm. A Cumberland sauce goes well with it.

MOUSSE OF HARE

8oz / 225g uncooked hare	10fl oz / 300ml double cream
1½ egg whites	Salt, pepper, nutmeg

Take the meat off the bone, strip it of all sinews and membranes. Add the egg whites and blend them for quite a long time in a food processor. Rub through a fine sieve. Gradually beat in the double cream and season the mixture well. Butter a terrine mould and spoon in the mousse. Cook in a cool oven, 140°C / 275°F / gas mark 1, the terrine in a water bath. It is cooked when firm and a needle comes out cleanly, after about three quarters of an hour.

This can be served hot, but it can be cooled as well and then cut into slices. You can also cook it as if it were a *quenelle*, placing spoonfuls into a pan of barely simmering water. When served hot, it goes well with a celeriac purée and some cranberries; when cold, a celery and apple salad.

These hot meat moulds are undeservedly neglected. There is a delicious chicken liver custard in Richard Olney's *Simple French Food* (1981) and there are other, simpler, recipes for *timbales* of chicken livers based on a flour-thickened *roux* which have their place as well. These are nice served with a Madeira sauce, which can work well with the mousse of hare, although the cranberries give a lift of sharpness to excite the appetite.

A FISH AND SCALLOP PÂTÉ

A modern form of scallop pâté is a purée of the fish, mixed with egg whites and cream, and set by gentle poaching in a water bath. This gives a very light result. Disaster can occur, normally in the middle of the full fury of service. If not adequately set, and the margin should be a fine one, the mousse is inedible and impossible to extract from its mould. The recipe below is cheaper, because it uses a combination of fish and scallops, and simpler to execute. The end product is firm, some might think too firm. The quantity is sufficient for a first course for six people.

4oz / 110g white fish (weighed off the bone and skinned)	Salt and pepper
4oz / 110g scallops	¾oz / 20g butter
10fl oz / 300ml milk	¾oz / 20g flour
5fl oz / 150ml double cream	Bay leaf, peppercorns, parsley stalks
3 sheets of gelatine	

Poach your fish, off the bone and skinned, in the milk with a bay leaf, peppercorns and parsley stalks. Any white fish will do, for instance hake or cod. Add the scallops towards the end of the poaching. The roes will give a nice glow to the colour.

Remove the fish when cooked. Strain the milk and make a *roux* with the butter, flour and milk. Cook out the flour. Soak the leaf gelatine in cold water. Put the fish and the *roux* through the liquidiser and season. Dissolve the gelatine in this warm purée. Lightly whip the double cream and stir into the pâté. Pour into a lined mould – for instance a loaf tin lined out with clingfilm. Leave to cool and set in a refrigerator. It will slice easily.

This is made more enjoyable by a raw sauce, perhaps made with tomatoes (with some vinegar to sharpen it) or from grated cucumber, dill and cream.

SALAMI, FROM BARRY MEHEW

The lot of anyone keeping house is lightened by enterprising retailers. Barry Mehew and Kate Gould keep the Delicatessen at Dartmouth and sell cheese, speciality groceries, *charcuterie* and their own cooked dishes. Acquaintance with them has been a constant pleasure and spur to extra effort. Barry Mehew is ever experimenting with his own *charcuterie* – sausages, dried hams and salamis. His salami, based on a reading of Jane Grigson's *Charcuterie and French Pork Cookery*, shows that such things may be made in our own homes with less fuss and bother than might at first be presumed.

2lb / 900g lean shoulder of pork	Some whole peppercorns
1lb / 450g lean chuck beef	2 teaspoons *quatre épices*
½lb / 225g hard pork fat	mixture
1 teaspoon saltpetre	1 teaspoon ground nutmeg
2oz / 50g sea salt	A glass of rum or brandy
2 teaspoons sugar	Garlic, puréed, to taste
1 teaspoon ground black pepper	Ox middles for skin

The pork and beef is chopped by hand into roughly bean-sized pieces, the pork fat a little smaller. Mix the lean meats in a bowl with the saltpetre and most of the salt and the sugar. Mix the pork fat with the rest of the salt and sugar in another bowl. The quantity of pork fat is up to you; the addition of more will tend to 'sweeten' the mixture. Place these bowls in the refrigerator overnight.

The next day tip them out on to a board and add all the spices and flavourings. (The *quatre épices* mixture can be bought from delicatessens.) You may care to soak some herbs in the brandy and add them too. The resultant mixture should then be stuffed as tightly as possible into ox middles. These are larger than pig's intestine and give a better-sized sausage. It took Barry some time to secure a supply, so you may have a lot of walking to do. Hang your salamis in a cool, well-ventilated space for six to eight weeks before consuming them. They should keep for six months.

When written down, it sounds easy, but having the determination to go through with it is something that many of us may lack.

Hot beginnings

NUT CROQUETTES WITH BEAN CURD, WITH AN ONION AND LEMON SAUCE

Colin Spencer's columns in the *Guardian* about vegetarian food and the food-supply establishment never fail to arouse us to comment if not action. These croquettes are an adaptation of one of his recipes. They were served with this lemon and onion sauce, also one of Colin Spencer's.

1 packet of bean curd or tofu
1oz / 25g butter
4oz / 110g onion
2oz / 50g butter
2oz / 50g flour
12fl oz / 360ml milk or
   vegetable stock
2 sheets of gelatine

4oz / 110g mixed chopped nuts
1 tablespoonful each poppy,
   sesame and mustard seeds
Seasoning
1oz / 25g flaked almonds
Dried bread crumbs
Egg wash

Drain the tofu on paper towels overnight. Chop the onion and sweat in one ounce of butter. When the onion is soft, set to one side. Make a roux with two ounces of butter and flour, adding milk or stock. Season, cook out and take off the heat. Add two soaked sheets of gelatine and stir to dissolve. Add the onions, nuts and the seeds. Check seasoning again. Spread on a tray and leave in the refrigerator to set completely.

Cut the bean curd into small batons. Take spoonfuls of the croquette mixture, flatten them out on a floured board and wrap them round each baton of curd. Chill. Mix the almonds with the crumbs. Dip the croquettes in egg wash then the crumbs. Deep fry on a low to medium heat until golden brown.

Onion and lemon sauce

1 large onion
½ lemon

1oz / 25g butter
Seasoning

Slice the onions thinly. Take the zest off the lemon with a potato peeler. Cook both in butter in a covered saucepan until soft and transparent – about ten minutes. Add lemon juice and some seasoning. Liquidise to a purée and serve.

SPINACH AND CREAM CHEESE PANCAKES

This uses the pancake batter described for strawberry pancakes on page 195. The pancakes are made and piled up ready for filling. Two pancakes (approximately 6in / 15cm) per person are needed for a first course.

1lb / 450g cleaned spinach   Salt, pepper, nutmeg
1oz / 25g butter   Single cream
8oz / 225g cream cheese

Cook the spinach with the butter in a covered saucepan. Purée it, either in a food mill, a processor or through the mincer. Mix it with cream cheese, season it quite highly. If it is too thick, let it down with a little single cream.

Put a dessertspoonful on each pancake and roll it up. To reheat, grease an oval dish and brush the pancakes with butter. Cover with foil and put in a moderate oven (190°C / 375°F / gas mark 5) for ten minutes. They can be tricky to reheat; a careful check should be made that they are thoroughly warmed.

STUFFED COURGETTE FLOWERS

16 courgette flowers   *Batter*
2oz / 50g onion
½oz / 15g butter   4oz / 110g flour
1 sheet gelatine   3 tablespoons olive oil
1oz / 25g flour   Water
1oz / 25g butter   1 egg white
5fl oz / 150ml milk
12oz cooked chicken, skinned
    and boned
Fresh tarragon

Make a *roux* with the flour, butter and milk. Chop and sweat the onion in butter. Soak the gelatine in cold water and squeeze dry. Add the onion to the *roux*, cook out and season.

Chop the chicken and the tarragon. Add, with the sheet of gelatine, to the *roux*, stir to dissolve the gelatine, check seasoning again and leave to cool.

Make the batter by combining the flour, oil and water to the consistency of a thin cream. It is best to leave this standing for an hour. Whisk the egg white stiffly and fold it in shortly before use. Ensure that it is well seasoned.

Put some of the mixture into each courgette flower and fold the petals over at the end. Dip in the batter and deep fry in comparatively cool oil for about three to four minutes, turning when brown. Drain on kitchen paper.

A PUFF PASTRY WITH QUAIL EGGS AND ASPARAGUS, WITH A HERB AND CREAM SAUCE

4oz / 100g puff pastry
1 bundle of asparagus
8 quail eggs

Herb and cream sauce
1 egg yolk
Lemon juice
White wine
3oz / 75g unsalted butter
Salt and cayenne
3fl oz / 90ml double cream
Chopped chervil, parsley and
    tarragon

Roll out the puff pastry very thinly; put on greased baking sheets and prick with a fork. Bake at 200°C / 400°F / gas mark 6 until golden. Divide into eight squares.

Prepare and cook the asparagus. This is eaten with a knife and fork, so none of it should be chewy or inedible. The jumbo asparagus from abroad can be peeled at the base to ensure that all is tender. Thinner English asparagus should be trimmed. It wants to be cooked just so. Times will range from above ten minutes for the very large that may have been picked for a few days, to five minutes for fresh, local, small spears.

The quail eggs are soft-boiled. Have some boiling water on the stove, immerse them for one minute in the bubbling pan, then refresh under cold water. This time will do for a dozen eggs; more than that and it will lengthen. Peel them gingerly. They can be warmed in water (that is not so hot as to cook them) when the time comes to serve them.

Make a *hollandaise* sauce. Over a double boiler, whisk an egg yolk, white wine and lemon juice until warm. Melt the butter. Whisk into the egg yolk, off the heat, to get an emulsion. Stir in the cream and the chopped herbs and bring back to temperature. Check seasoning. Do not overheat.

The assembly needs everything hot. The pastry may have been made earlier, it can be reheated in a moderate to cool oven. Asparagus does not reheat well; nor will the sauce. Place a square of puff paste on a plate; put on some asparagus, two soft quail eggs and a spoonful of sauce. Crown with another square of puff paste and some more sauce.

TART OF QUAIL EGGS WITH MUSHROOMS AND TARRAGON CREAM

This is a derivative of that famous dish found at the Connaught Hotel. There, tiny *oeufs mollets* of the quail eggs are made, set upon a *duxelles* within the lightest of pastry boats and topped with a *hollandaise* sauce. The present recipe is more suited to the home table or rustic bench. For a first course for four people, you need:

Four 4in / 10cm tart cases of the lightest and thinnest of short crust, baked blind
2oz / 50g shallot
8oz / 225g button mushrooms
1oz / 25g butter

Single cream
Salt, pepper and nutmeg
8 quail eggs
4fl oz / 120ml double cream
Sprig of tarragon
Salt and pepper

Peel and chop the shallot finely. Wipe the mushrooms clean; the best buttons will give you the palest colour and a light flavour. Slice them. Sweat the onion in butter and add the mushrooms. Keep cooking, but not too long. Put the whole into a blender or processor and blend to a purée. Add a dash of single cream to keep the consistency workable. Taste and season with salt, pepper and nutmeg.

Heat the tart cases briefly in the oven. Heat the mushroom purée. Divide it between the cases, piling it more thickly round the perimeter so as to give a declivity for the eggs and cream in the centre. Break two quail eggs into each hollow. Use a serrated knife to crack the shells; they are surprisingly tough. Season with salt and pepper. Bake the tarts for two minutes in a hot oven (200°C / 400°F / gas mark 6), then add a small spoonful of seasoned double cream mixed with chopped tarragon. Bake for another two minutes.

SPICED CHICKEN CROQUETTES

This recipe uses the three spices cumin, coriander and cardamom. Its technique is similar to that described for fish cakes on page 154. It is an excellent way of using left-over chicken and making a substantial first course or a lunch or supper dish.

12oz / 325g cooked chicken
  meat, off the bone
4oz / 110g onion
1oz / 25g butter
½ teaspoon each of cumin and
  coriander
8 cardamom pods

2 sheets of gelatine
2oz / 50g butter
2oz / 50g flour
13fl oz / 390ml milk
Salt, pepper, egg wash, dried
  crumbs

Peel and finely chop the onion. Sweat it in butter without taking colour. Deseed the cardamom and grind the spices in a coffee mill or pestle and mortar. Add them to the onion and fry a little longer.

Remove any skin from the chicken and chop finely.

Make a *roux* of the butter, flour and milk. Add the onion and spices and season well. Take off the heat. Add the soaked sheets of gelatine, stir and dissolve in the *roux*. Stir in the chicken and check the seasoning.

Spread the resultant mixture on a tray. Cover with clingfilm to prevent a skin forming and refrigerate. When it is thoroughly cold and set, shape it into croquettes (if deep fried) or patties (if shallow fried). Dip in flour, egg and dry bread crumbs. The croquettes should be about an inch in diameter and two inches long.

These are cooked at 170°C–180°C / 325°F–350°F in a deep fryer for about three minutes. They, like the fish cakes, will burst if the fat is too hot. Shallow fried, they will take three to four minutes each side over a medium heat. A celery and watercress salad and a spiced lemon pickle are good accompaniments.

Fish

FISH CAKES OR SALMON AND MUSHROOM CUTLETS

This is a recipe that was first laid down for salmon and mushroom cutlets. It is an excellent way of using the bits and pieces from the head and tail. The budgetary limits of the Tall Ships as well as a requirement to consume quantities of fish before it went out of condition, turned it from salmon and mushroom cutlets to fish cakes. The English fish-cake mixture using fluffy mashed potato or bread crumbs as a filler and binder can be unsatisfactory. This way of doing it is first rate. What is more, the cakes can be made, shaped up, crumbed, then frozen. To cook a 2oz / 50g cake from frozen, you need oil at 170°C / 325°F for six minutes.

12oz / 325g cooked fish, off the bone	13fl oz / 390ml milk
	2 sheets gelatine
4oz / 110g onion	Lemon juice
2oz / 50g butter	Salt and pepper
8oz / 220g mushrooms	Egg wash
2oz / 50g flour	Dried crumbs

Poach your fish in milk, take it off the bone and flake it. The species is immaterial so long as it is white fish. If you are using up salmon, then it may well be poached already. Use the poaching milk (probably seasoned with a bay leaf, celery and peppercorns) as the liquid for the *roux*.

Peel and chop the onions and slice the mushrooms. Sweat first the onion, then the mushrooms in butter.

Make a *roux* of the flour, butter and milk. Soak the gelatine in cold water. When the flour has cooked out, add the onions and mushrooms and allow to cool a little before adding the soaked gelatine. Stir to dissolve. Add the flaked fish and check the seasoning. It should be quite well seasoned.

Spread the warm mixture on to a tray to cool completely in the refrigerator and to set. Eventually, it should be very stiff indeed. After an hour or two in the fridge, if not longer, divide into 2oz / 50g portions which can be shaped roughly before flouring, egging and crumbing with home-made, dried crumbs. This is a messy and thankless task for which three pairs of hands are better than one. If the shape is reasonable before the egg-wash stage, it is not too bad to pat into a perfect cake after crumbing. Whether they are in a cutlet shape or circular, they taste the same and cook the same.

It is at this point they can be frozen. Easiest is to leave them on a clean tray, then pack them into bags or boxes after they have frozen.

To cook them from fresh, use a fairly cool oil (160°–180°C / 325°–360°F) for three or four minutes until the crumbs have browned. We have always deep fried but shallow frying is equally efficient. They are susceptible to bursts, particularly if the mixture is not stiff enough or if subjected to too intense a heat during the final cooking. Drain on kitchen paper.

These are surprisingly rich: two for a first course, three for a main course. They need a sauce: tomato, tartare, herb and cream.

DOVER SOLE ON A BED OF LEEKS, STUFFED WITH LANGOUSTINE AND SCALLOPS, WITH A LANGOUSTINE SAUCE

The quantities here are for a generous double portion. It might be spread among three people, but only between four or six as a first course.

1 Dover sole, about 20oz / 550g	Grated zest of lemon
3 scallops	2oz / 50g butter
The tails of ten langoustines	2fl oz / 60ml white wine
1 leek	

Skin the sole. Strip out the backbone. If you find this complicated, you can fillet it. The langoustines must also be dealt with, live if possible. Pinch the bottoms of the tail shells together to loose them, then prize them apart with the finger nails, removing them from the tail flesh. Holding the head and claws in one hand and the tail in the other, pull apart. If lucky, the black vein will go with the head. If it does not, it may be extracted by cutting finely down the back and picking it out.

Stuff the sole or layer the fillets with a mixture of the tails, sliced muscle (not roe) of scallop, salt, pepper and a very little grated zest of lemon. Slice the leek very finely, arrange as a bed in an ovenproof dish, add the melted butter and white wine. Place the sole atop this, seasoning the whole. Cover with foil and cook in a very slow oven until just done.

In the meanwhile, make a sauce.

Half an onion
Top end of a leek
1 carrot
Heads and shells of langoustines
Butter, thyme, marjoram

Sweat the vegetables, add the langoustines, fry some more. Bash vigorously with a rolling pin. Add the herbs, cover with water and simmer until a strong decoction results.

1 giant beefsteak tomato
Dessertspoon of chopped chives
1oz / 25g butter

Peel and deseed tomato. Cook with butter until a purée. Add the langoustine stock and the white wine juices from the cooking of the sole. Reduce until satisfactory, then add the roes from the scallops, in thick slices. Finish with butter and seasoning.

DOVER SOLE *AU VERT*

20oz / 550g fillets of Dover sole	Flour, salt and pepper
(5oz / 140g per person)	Lemon juice
4oz / 10g butter	
Sorrel, parsley, chervil,	
lemon thyme	

The simplest way with summer sole. Fillet and skin the fish; score the inner membrane to prevent twisting and curling. Season them, dust them with flour. Wash, strip and chop the herbs. A lot of sorrel, not much lemon thyme. It is best to be generous.

Put the butter in a large, good, frying pan, for preference not aluminium. Clarified butter, i.e. that which has been melted and poured off its whey, performs better. Over a high heat, fry the sole, allowing it to take colour. Remove to a serving dish, squeeze half a lemon over it. Turn back to the cooking pan. Throw in the herbs and cook without burning. Pour over the fish.

FILLETS OF DOVER SOLE IN A LETTUCE LEAF

There has ever been a harmless passion for making little parcels of things, and wrapping in a vegetable leaf is a good way of introducing the flavour without overpowering the contents. Lettuce has come into vogue with the dishes of some French chefs, the most famous recipe being, perhaps, Roger Vergé's sea bass in lettuce leaves, of which this is a lighter version. It is another way of using slip soles. The quantities below are for four people.

20oz / 350g fillets of Dover sole	The outer leaves of a Webb's
4oz / 110g shallot	lettuce
5fl oz / 150ml white vermouth	2oz / 50g butter

Chop the shallot and put in a pan with the vermouth. Reduce the liquid by half by boiling. Blanch the outer leaves of the lettuce very briefly in boiling water, drain and refresh under the cold tap. Spread them on a board.

Skin the fillets and score the inner membrane lightly before rolling each of them, skin side inside. The scoring is done to prevent them from uncurling in the heat. Season them. Place each little fillet, or two if they are very tiny, on a lettuce leaf and fold over to make a parcel.

In a small ovenproof dish, lay out the shallot and vermouth reduction and put your parcels on top. Cover with foil. Bring up to heat on the top, then cook in a cool oven (150°C / 300°F / gas mark 2) for about five minutes. Remove the parcels to a warm place and bring the reduction back to the top of the stove. There, shuffle in a few pats of butter, taste, season with lemon juice and pour over the fillets.

GOUJONS OF DOVER SOLE WITH CHAMPAGNE

The price of Dover sole, never low, should depend on its size. The small and the large are cheaper than the prime weighing 12–16oz / 340–450g. Slip soles will have less flavour and will be softer; the giants will taste excellent but may be on the firm side. Aberrant sizes makes it more difficult to serve a single fish per portion and thus some form of division, either by filleting or by cutting into still smaller pieces like *goujons*, is required. This recipe, calling for *goujons*, also needs scraps of champagne – a requirement more easily fulfilled in a restaurant than a private house. White wine can be used instead.

Fillet and skin the sole. Cut the fillets into diagonal strips the size of a little finger. Dust them with flour, salt and pepper. Fry them rapidly in butter, allowing the flour to take colour and cook out. Remove them from the pan on to a serving dish and squeeze some lemon juice on them before reserving in the warm. Add a little more butter to the pan and let it foam but not burn. Swoosh in a glass or half a glass of champagne, on a high heat by now, and let it reduce a little. Add a lot of chopped parsley and pour over the fish. The whole process takes two and a half minutes.

For a first course, 2–3oz / 50–75g of fish per person; for a main course, between 4–6oz / 110–160g. Remember when buying the fish that half the gross weight may be lost in filleting and skinning. I do not think it worth trying such a dish with a softer fish like lemon sole or plaice. The *goujons*, so handled, will not stand up to it.

LEMON SOLE WITH VIRGIN OIL

Like many recipes, this came to light in a waiting room while running through magazines. The reader was my mother-in-law; she cooked it for us when organising the household after the birth of our daughter. It seemed to solve the problem of the lemon sole: that all too often it lacks taste and texture. The method is a peasant version of the original.

Take a 14oz / 400g fish per person and trim it of its skirt and tail. Do not skin it. Lay it, white side uppermost, under a grill having *liberally* anointed it with salt. Cook on a moderate heat until the skin is burnt and blistered (about five minutes); turn it over and, after another liberal salting, repeat the process on the black skin. Put the fish on to plates or a serving dish and dress with the best extra-virgin oil mixed with chopped parsley. This can be warmed before application. Serve with lemon. The aroma of the oil and the crispness of the salted skin combine to enhance the flesh.

TURBOT WITH LIME AND GREEN GINGER

4 turbot fillets, each about 6oz / 160g	1 teaspoon grated fresh ginger
	1oz / 25g butter
1 lime	2fl oz / 60ml white wine

Peel and grate the ginger on the coarse grater. Pare the lime in strips, without the pith, and blanch them in plain water. Remove the pith from the lime itself and cut the fruit into sections. Shred the blanched peel very finely.

Put the turbot fillets on a buttered dish, arrange the lime sections on top, spread the grated ginger as well and add the blanched peel. Season with salt and pepper and add the wine. Bring to the boil on the top and transfer to a cool oven (130°C / 250°F / gas mark ½), covered with foil, until the fillets are cooked.

This may be finished either by reducing the juices, or by coating with a *hollandaise*, whose unctuousness is enjoyable in contrast to the taste of ginger and lime.

This calls for turbot. You could use cod or hake. It would be less satisfactory with one of the cheaper flat fishes such as lemon sole or plaice. If using anything less firm than turbot, the temperature of the oven and the timing of the cooking has to be watched very carefully. Too hot and it will cook before you have time to turn around; far better at a low setting, having taken the pan to a good heat on the top to begin with.

STEAMED TURBOT

This came about with the purchase of a set of bamboo stacking steamers and is the sort of dish that fits uneasily into our repertoire. Nonetheless, it was very enjoyable and very easy to effect.

1lb / 450g turbot fillet
1 teaspoon chopped green ginger

4oz / 110g each of red pimento, yellow pimento, spinach, carrot, mooli, French beans
6oz / 160g soft Chinese noodles

Skin the turbot fillets and slice the flesh into thin strips. Mix them with the chopped green ginger and turn them in some oil.

Cook the soft noodles. Drain them and set aside. Slice all the vegetables extremely thinly.

Arrange each ingredient on a plate, cover it with clingfilm and place it inside a bamboo steamer. Pile these on to the pan containing water over which you are going to steam them. The fish to go in the middle of the pile, and the noodles at the top. Steam for about eight minutes. Length will depend on the size of the strips, as well as the efficiency with which you can fit your steamer to the water pan beneath. Unpack and arrange on a serving dish.

We served this with a green coriander leaf sauce described by Nathalie Hambro in *Particular Delights* (1981), one of the great modern cookery books. It is an emulsion of coriander leaves, French mustard, oil and vinegar, achieved in the blender.

MONKFISH WITH CRAB AND GREEN GINGER

A large tail of monkfish, about   2oz / 50g butter
    2lb / 900g   2fl oz / 60ml white wine
6oz / 160g white crab meat   Fresh coriander
1 tablespoon grated green ginger

Skin the monkfish tail; the large fish have a better texture than the small.
Take each fillet off the central bone. Remove the subcutaneous mem-
brane which, if left intact, may cause the flesh to pucker in the cooking.
Allow six ounces of boned and skinned fish per person.

Dress the crab meat with pepper, lemon juice and salt (if necessary)
and mix with the peeled and grated ginger. Slice the monkfish into thin
escalopes and arrange in a dish in which the butter has been melted,
interleaving the slices with the crab and ginger. Pour over the wine,
bring to the boil and finish cooking covered with foil in a cool oven
(130°C / 250°F / gas mark ½).

Remove the fish on to a serving dish, boil up the pan juices to reduce
somewhat and finish with cream or butter. Strew chopped coriander
leaves before sending forth.

COULIBIAC OF SALMON

Or, perhaps, *Kulebyaka s Vyazigoi*. We thought to cook this dish for a
subscription dinner; we have wrapped so much salmon in pastry with
ginger and currants, for so long, that a change was good for us.

Recipes are legion, from Petit's *La Gastronomie en Russie*, to
Countess Morphy, Jacques le Divellec, Constance Spry, Jane Grigson
and Alan Davidson. They range from the simple – Arabella Boxer uses
short crust, rice, herbs and eggs – to the lengthy, with brains, buckwheat, *vesiga,* eggs, dill and yeast doughs. In Gogol's *Dead Souls*, the
town of Torzhok had a splendid fish market and the offerings of an
impromptu feast included 'white sturgeon, ordinary sturgeon, salmon,
pressed caviare, fresh caviare, herrings, stellated sturgeon, cheeses of all
sorts, smoked tongue, and dried sturgeon – all this came from the fish
market. Then there appeared all sorts of supplementary dishes from the
kitchen: a pie made with the head, gristle and cheeks of a three hundred
pound sturgeon, another pie stuffed with mushrooms, fried pastries,
dumplings cooked in melted butter, and fruit stewed in honey.' How
different from a buffet that might have been arrayed in an English
country town of the same era.

The reference to gristle in the giant sturgeon pie must be to *vesiga* –

the cartilaginous knobs from the backbone of a sturgeon that are dried and then reconstituted for use in this dish and which are much prized for their texture and taste. It can be bought in speciality shops, in a box devoid of any language but Russian, and we followed the experts' advice for dealing with it, first soaking it for two hours and then cooking it for half an hour. We found it still knobbly and gritty, so extended the times. This was some improvement. The best is to soak it overnight and to boil it for several hours. This will then give it the glutinous texture that is required. The recipe we followed was a hybrid, more complex than is either our wont or that of most domestic cooks. However, the end product is very satisfying, is far removed from the normal *coulibiac* of pastry, mushroom and eggs and may justify the pains.

The first stage is the dough. For this we used a croissant yeast dough, i.e. very flaky and buttery. It is possible to use a flaky pastry, very much simpler of execution, or a choux paste or a brioche dough.

8oz / 225g flour	5fl oz / 150ml milk
8oz / 225g butter	¼ teaspoon salt
½oz / 15g yeast	¼ teaspoon sugar

Cream the milk, sugar and yeast. Mix with the flour and salt. Leave to rest for fifteen minutes in the cool. Roll out into a strip twice as long as it is wide. Spread the butter in flakes over half the strip, fold over the other half, press down at the edges and roll out to the original size. This process of rolling, folding and rolling is repeated three times, six rolls in all, resting for fifteen minutes in the cool between alternate turns. This makes a very well-behaved dough. It held round the filling with sufficient strength for carving both hot and cold. Yet it was not stodgy. It also baked crisp on the bottom, where it soaked up much of the juice from the pie; this was enjoyable to eat. Next, the filling:

1lb / 450g boned and skinned salmon (i.e. a piece weighing approximately 2lb / 900g in the unbutchered state)	4oz / 110g chopped onion
	6oz / 160g butter
	1oz / 25g dried *vesiga*
	2oz / 50g buckwheat
2 chopped hard boiled eggs	2 tablespoons chopped fresh dill
Juice of half a lemon	Fish stock or water
8oz / 225g sliced mushrooms	

Cook the buckwheat (obtainable from health food stores) in a little fish stock or water and drain. Soak the *vesiga* and cook in fresh water. Sweat the onion in three ounces of butter, add the mushrooms and cook for five minutes. Melt the rest of the butter and mix with the eggs and the dill. Season each of these ingredients.

Prepare your salmon, making two large fillets. To bone a salmon the backbone has to be removed, easy enough, but the lateral bones, severed from the backbone when the fish is filleted, also have to be taken out. For this, a pair of pliers is the best tool. Many recipes suggest that the fish is seared in butter before being put into the pie, and broken into large flakes. There is nothing to be gained by this.

On a floured table, roll the dough into a large oblong. Spread upon it one third of the *vesiga*, egg mixture and mushroom. Place one of the fillets upon this bed. Season the fillet. Put a second layer of the mixtures atop the fillet followed by the second fillet. Finally, dispose of the rest of the mixtures on top of this and compact the whole with your hands. Fold the dough over, with a good overlap. Turn the parcel so that the seam is on the bottom. If there is surplus paste, make a head and tail to the pie once it is in position on the greased baking sheet. Egg wash all over. Using a sharp blade, make crescent-shaped incisions over the top – this to simulate scales – and make some deeper cuts to allow for the escape of steam.

This may be baked in a hot oven (230°C / 450°F / gas mark 8) for thirty minutes. If the pastry colours too much, then the heat should be reduced after fifteen minutes. To eat, serve it with wedges of lemon and some sour cream. It is important that the filling should be moist and succulent. Using *vesiga* is one answer, the butter is essential, but brains might well be substituted for the *vesiga* if its location proved insuperable. It is also important not to overcook the fish. As the dish eats very well cold, keeping the flesh moist and only just cooked become more important.

HOME-SMOKED FISH: GURNARD AND SPRATS

The operation of a smoker is so simple and the end result such a change from normal tastes that one is surprised it is not more popular as a means of cooking. There is no need to invest time or money in major construction projects, beloved of do-it-yourself authors anxious that you should smoke whole herds of reindeer, shoals of salmon or flocks of turkeys. A simple home smoker that may double as a charcoal grill can be purchased for not many pounds. The tiny Swedish box smokers seem too small to be practicable, but this may reflect our limited experience. While accepting and endorsing the smoking of fish, I have never been so enamoured of smoking meat. There is rarely any oiliness to counteract, nor taste to buttress and reinforce. The process of producing hams I leave to larger-scale operations than ours.

The hot smoking described here does not preserve. The fish needs to be consumed within a day or two, just as if it were fresh. It can, however, be reheated without damage. Thus the smoking may be done in the day, the fish refrigerated under cover, then put in a very cool oven before being served.

Gurnard is extremely cheap. Its flesh can be moist and dense, if it is fresh, but there is an inherent danger of woolliness and dryness if condition is not tip-top. It may be thought a good vehicle for some fairly radical cooking to overcome any deficiencies. The smoker thus comes into its own. Fillet the gurnard to give two large fillets, each weighing about eight ounces. If you have smaller fish, the timing will be proportionately reduced. Soak the fish in salt water for half an hour, dabbing it dry with a cloth or paper when you remove it. In the meantime, light the fire in the smoker and add two cupfuls of soaked hickory chips. Put the fillets on the smoking grid, with a bowl of water beneath, cover the machine with its lid and leave for two hours. This will give a gentle smoke, just cooked, but no more.

The fish can be consumed there and then. Or it can be left to cool and served as a salad. Or it can be reheated in the oven. The bowl of water in the smoker can be rescued and its contents reduced over heat to give you a barbecue sauce. This can be brushed, in moderation, on the fillets as they are reheated. Two accompaniments are satisfactory: the first a cucumber and sour cream mixture, the second a raw tomato sauce.

Sprats are another south-western fish that is a candidate for the smoker. At the end of the year, the boats begin to catch them in very large numbers. The majority are exported. For a week or two, almost the only thing landed on Brixham quay is box after box of sprats. They are delicious to eat but the glut forces the cook to seek varied and interesting ways to present them. Yet their size militates against elaboration, and their oiliness against refinement. The one advantage a seaside kitchen has over the rest of the country is that the produce will be fresh: a signal fact.

Sprats may be pickled. This was the procedure with the vast catches of pelagic fish that used to be taken by seine netting on the Devon and Cornish coasts: pilchards, sprats, small herrings. The fish are soaked in vinegar overnight, drained, then layered in crocks or jars with a mixture made of two parts sea salt to one part sugar, fortified with crushed black pepper, bruised allspice and bay leaves. Leave such small fish in their covered jars for about three weeks and they are ready to consume.

Another mode of presentation is the smoker. It counteracts the richness of the fish. Preparations for the machine are the same as for the gurnard; however, the temptation to leave the sprats whole should be resisted. Troublesome as it is, they do better with the backbone removed. After that, the smoking is a very quick job, no more than twenty minutes.

A CRUDE AND SIMPLE GARLIC AND PIMENTO SAUCE FOR FISH

Food needs to delight, it needs to nourish and it needs to stimulate a jaded body or head into a semblance of action. The Prairie Oyster style of cooking may be crude but it has its place. This sauce ranks therein. It can accompany a piece of fish stewed with tomato and white wine.

1 onion
3 large cloves of garlic
7oz / 200g tin of red pimentoes

1 or 2 chilli peppers, depending on strength

Chop the onion and the garlic. Sweat the onion without colouring in a strong olive oil. Add the garlic at the end of this process. Drain the pimentoes and chop. Add them. Chop the chilli, deseeded, and stir it in. Season with salt.

FENNEL AND LEEK CREAM FOR GRILLED FISH

When bass is brought in during the summer one has almost a knee-jerk response: grill it with lemon and herbs; send it out with perhaps an *aïoli* or a mayonnaise with chilli or a *rouille*. Such dishes, one's natural assumptions, raise the question of fashion and innovation. For this mode really does appear to be one of the best ways of dealing with sea bass or other grilled fish. So good is it that it may seem hackneyed. Yet the vast majority of customers will have not eaten anything like it for months, if not years, before they come to Dartmouth. Most, after all, will not have visited a seaside restaurant in that time. Is it worth, therefore, casting around for some novel mode of cooking? Familiarity breeds disdain and while we on one side of the stove think that all is repetitious, it is not so to the rest of the world. Novelty is often sought where quality would suffice. To have the two together may be a bonus, but such even-handedness is rare.

Sea bass, however, is also caught when herbs are dormant and other flavours must be brought into play. Thus a winter grilled bass can be well accompanied by two sauces: one a hot concoction from Tarragona, balanced by the other, a cream of fennel and leeks. The Tarragona sauce, *romescu*, is described in many works, few better than Arabella Boxer's *Mediterranean Cookbook* (1981). A mixture of dried chilli, almonds, pine kernels, garlic, tomato and oil, it is to be recommended. Tom Stobart would say that the substitution of normal dried chilli for the not so hot *romescu* pepper used in Spain is a serious error. This combination surfaces again in Spanish dishes for salt cod and tripe; both first class ways of dealing with difficult subjects.

To counteract the heat of the chilli, a fennel and leek cream is excellent.

1 Florentine fennel	Butter
Single cream	Salt, pepper and lemon juice
2 leeks	

Boil the bulb of fennel until tender, pass it through the food mill or food processor and then a fine sieve. Add single cream, about 50 per cent of the volume of fennel, and a purée of leeks that have been finely sliced, sweated in butter and similarly milled and sieved. Check for seasoning.

Shellfish

LOBSTER WITH LETTUCE, VERMOUTH AND CREAM

This was done as a first course, using the lobster tail. The claws were put to another dish.

1 lobster tail from a 24oz / 675g fish
Half an onion
1 cabbage lettuce

2oz / 50g butter
Small glass dry vermouth
2fl oz / 60ml double cream
1 egg yolk

Cut the lobster tail into collops. Chop the onion and sweat in butter. Shred the lettuce and add that. Add the vermouth and the lobster tail. Cook. Remove the lobster, reduce the liquid, add a liaison of cream and egg yolk, allow to thicken without boiling, otherwise the egg will scramble. Taste for seasoning and lemon juice, pour over lobster.

AN ENGLISH DRESSING FOR A LOBSTER

There are occasions when one pines for something more brutal to accompany a cold lobster than vinaigrette or mayonnaise. This is a variation on a hard-boiled egg dressing.

2 hard-boiled eggs
Handful of sorrel
½oz / 12g butter
1 teaspoon Dijon mustard

Anchovy sauce
2fl oz / 60ml olive oil
½fl oz / 15ml wine vinegar
Salt and pepper

Wash, strip and sweat the sorrel in the butter. Chop the eggs finely. Stir the sorrel into the eggs, add the mustard and a bit of anchovy sauce. Put in the vinegar, then beat in the oil. Season. A fair emulsion is achieved. It can be used as a dressing for vegetables.

LOBSTER *MALLORQUINA*

The quantities are for six people.

3 lobsters, each 1½lb / 675g	Lemon juice, salt and pepper
1oz / 25g butter	2oz / 50g butter
1oz / 25g flour	4fl oz / 120ml dry sherry
10fl oz / 300ml single cream	Brandy
2fl oz / 60ml dry sherry	5 eggs

Boil the lobsters and split them lengthways. Remove the flesh from the tails, claws and heads. Keep the claw meat whole. Reserve the body and tail shells. Make a *roux* of the butter, flour and single cream. Cook it out, add the sherry, lemon juice and generous seasoning and leave off the heat.

Take the flesh of the lobster, cut the tails into collops and heat it very gently in butter with sherry on top of the stove. Too fierce a heat will toughen it. In the meantime, heat up the shells, sprinkled with a little sherry, in a very cool oven. Flame the meat with some brandy and place it in the shells.

Separate the eggs. Add the yolks to the *roux* and beat the whites stiffly. Fold them into the thick base. Spoon this mixture on top of the lobster meat, trying to keep it tidily within the shells. Place in a hot oven (225°C / 450°F / gas mark 8), for about twelve to fifteen minutes. They should have risen up as soufflés and be nicely browned on top. The mixture will defend the lobster flesh from too much toughening from the heat.

PRAWNS WITH MANGO AND HORSERADISH

8oz / 225g prawns in the shell	1 teaspoon grated horseradish
4oz / 225g prepared mango	Sugar, lemon juice, single cream
2oz / 110g lemon mayonnaise	and seasoning

Shell the prawns. Grate the horseradish (which should be fresh). Mix it with the mayonnaise (which should be home-made) and a little single cream, adjusting the flavour with lemon and sugar, salt and pepper. The consistency should be binding. Peel the mango, which should be ripe, and cut into small cubes. Mix the three ingredients lightly. Serve with a salad of leaves and lettuces.

SCALLOPS WITH A PURÉE OF SPINACH AND MUSHROOM

Extremely rich, but very easy as a beginning. The combination of spinach and mushroom is tantalising – neither one thing nor the other.

4oz / 110g spinach	Sprig of thyme
4oz / 110g mushrooms	Lemon juice
2oz / 50g butter	Nutmeg, salt and pepper
12 scallops	A *beurre blanc*

Wash, strip and sweat the spinach with 1oz / 25g of butter. Blend it and reserve. Wipe, slice and sweat the mushrooms with the rest of the butter. Blend them and mix with the spinach. Season to taste: salt, pepper, nutmeg and lemon.

Fill a saucepan with water, put in a good sprig of thyme and bring to the boil. Over this steam the scallops, whole, very gently until they are just cooked. This allows three scallops per person.

Serve with the purée, seasoning the scallops with lemon juice and black pepper. Serve, if you wish, with a *beurre blanc*.

The proportions of a *beurre blanc* are simple: 2 shallots, 2 tablespoons of white wine vinegar, 2 tablespoons of white wine and 4oz / 110g of unsalted butter. Chop the shallot finely, reduce it with the vinegar and white wine until almost dry. Cut the butter into thin slices and add it gradually to the shallots, stirring or whisking all the time – off the heat so that the butter melts to a creamy whiteness, not a clear grease. The latter will occur if the pan gets too hot, so revisits to the flame (necessary so as to maintain some heat) should be as short as possible. Some people strain this sauce; it is quite unnecessary. You may feel it needs some seasoning, usually very little, if any. It can be kept warm on the back of the stove (not hot or it will break). Equally it can be brought back from the grave if it gets too cold. However, it is much easier to make it when you need it. The reduction can be prepared beforehand and the rest is rapid though heart-stopping.

Poultry and game

BREAST OF CHICKEN COOKED WITH PUFFBALLS

Puffballs have a good flavour, the small and the large, giant ones. Sometimes they need skinning as the outside is tough. Two small fungi are sufficient for one portion, or one or two slices of the giant, cut thick enough so that they keep their texture.

Take off the bone and skin a breast of chicken per person. Season it, fry it gently in clarified butter in a pan that can be covered later. Turn it when it takes colour. When turned, and coloured the other side, lay the slices of puffball on top, season them and cover the pan. Place it in a moderate oven (180°C / 350°F / gas mark 4) for fifteen minutes until cooked. Check it for completion at the wing joint.

Remove the chicken to a warm dish and deglaze the pan with a tablespoon of dry sherry per portion and two tablespoons of double cream. Reduce until thick, check the seasoning, adding lemon juice if required. Pour over the meat.

POACHED CHICKEN WITH A CELERIAC AND LEMON SAUCE

1 large chicken	1½oz / 40g butter
1 onion	1½oz / 40g flour
2 carrots	4oz celeriac, peeled
3 sticks of celery	Half a lemon
Stock herbs	5fl oz / 150ml double cream

Make a stock with the giblets, feet, winglets and neck of the chicken, an onion, two carrots, celery and stock herbs. Cool and skim.

Truss the chicken and place in a capacious pan, covering it with the stock. Bring it to the boil and simmer gently for between 45 minutes and one hour. Remove it from the stock and keep it warm.

Skim the stock of all fat, bring it back to the boil and strain it through a muslin. Take 2pts / 1.2l and reduce by boiling to 1pt / 60ml. Make a velouté with the butter, flour and reduced stock.

Take the celeriac, slice it and boil it in salted water until tender. Drain and put it through the fine plate of a food mill or a fine sieve. Add this to the *velouté*, together with the grated rind and juice of half a lemon. Taste and season. Make sure the flour has completely cooked out. Add the double cream and taste again. This is a sauce that may verge on the bland if not seasoned correctly. To serve, carve the chicken and coat with the sauce. Send up a selection of plain boiled vegetables.

QUAIL LEGS WITH SESAME SEEDS AND A LEMON SAUCE

Restaurants delight in offering dishes made up of halves of one raw commodity. It appeals to the economical: two items for one purchase. It has (especially with poultry) roots in reality. Legs and breasts are very different meats; their cooking demands different techniques and times. (Of course with tiny birds such as quail this is less true.) Being good for restaurants does not necessarily put it out of bounds for private houses. Attacking the raw material twice may cause more cooking, but it gives more mileage than eating endless cold cuts.

Take off your quail legs and marinate them in the following mixture for one hour:

1 egg white
1 tablespoon cornflour   1 tablespoon grated green ginger
1 tablespoon lemon juice   1 teaspoon soy sauce
1 tablespoon dry sherry   Salt and pepper

Remove them from the marinade and coat them on both sides with sesame seeds. Fry them gently, turning once, in either olive oil or nut oil, for four to six minutes. They should not take a great deal of cooking. Serve with a sauce made from the following:

3 tablespoons bitter orange   1 teaspoon cornflour, slaked in
    marmalade   1 tablespoon of cold water
2 cloves garlic   4fl oz / 120ml lemon juice
1 teaspoon grated lemon rind   Salt and pepper

Chop the garlic and fry gently in oil. Add the rest of the ingredients and cook out.

Serve with a few stir-fried Chinese leaves to give a little bulk.

LEGS OF DUCK WITH APRICOTS AND A SULTANA AND BRANDY SAUCE

4 duck legs	10fl oz / 300ml red wine
The livers of two ducks	½oz / 15g butter
4 fresh apricots	½oz / 15g flour
2fl oz / 60ml dry sherry	1 tablespoon sultanas
2oz / 50g butter	1fl oz / 30ml brandy
10fl oz / 300ml duck stock	

Take the legs off the carcases and remove any excess subcutaneous fat, while leaving the skins on. De-bone the thighs by making an incision along their length and scraping the flesh free of the bone then cutting through the joint. Do not puncture the skin.

Quarter the apricots, remove and crack the stones and chop the kernels. Marinate the kernels and fruit in sherry for half an hour. Then lay the fruit in the cavities in the thighs and sew up the pocket with a needle and thread. Season and brown the joints in butter.

Put them into a casserole with duck stock, red wine and seasoning. Bring to the boil, cover and cook in a cool oven for at least one hour until tender (130°C / 250°F / gas mark ½). Put to cool, remove all the fat, draw the threads from the legs and put them into a clean serving dish.

By boiling, reduce the cooking liquid by half and skim well. Thicken it with the small quantity of butter and flour. Marinate the sultanas in the brandy for an hour and add them to the sauce. Check the seasoning and pour it over the legs. Reheat very gently for half an hour.

This can be served with *croûtons* fried in duck fat, spread with the livers that have been cooked lightly in butter and moistened with sherry.

DUCK BREASTS WITH BLACKCURRANTS

Duck is often more suited to jointing and then separate cooking of the breasts and the legs than to simple roasting or boiling as a whole. It is true the extravagance of buying *two* ducks to feed four people (twice) will seem daunting at the outset; but then think of the stock and by-products – the ancillary meals that you may get out of them. For some time Muscovy ducks have been most often used in our kitchen. Their flesh is darker than Aylesburys, their body smaller. There is less fat.

4 duck breasts (each weighing about 4oz / 110g)	3oz / 75g butter
4oz / 110g blackcurrants	Brandy
10fl oz / 300ml duck stock	Seasoning

Take the breasts off the ducks and skin them. Leave the wing up to the first joint. Make a good stock with the carcases (having first removed the legs and other trimmings), less the liver.

Season the breasts and fry them lightly in butter on both sides so that they do not colour. Cover the pan and cook in a cool oven (140°C / 275°F / gas mark 1) for fifteen minutes. At that weight, with this timing, they should still be pink. Bring out on top of the stove and add the blackcurrants, washed and rid of their stalks. Flame with brandy. Reserve the breasts in the warm and add the stock to the pan. Reduce until you have a thick syrup. Taste for seasoning. The sauce may be finished with butter or left as it is. Carve the breasts and serve on the sauce.

POACHED BREAST OF PHEASANT WITH MORELS

If 'pillows' are extravagant of time while economical of materials, this way of dealing with pheasant is the opposite. It is cooked with morels, the next best thing after truffles; they can be bought dried, at great expense. It may be possible to use chanterelles, which are more readily found fresh, if mushroom hunter you are, or the dried Italian ceps, *boletus edulis*. These are more fragrant than cultivated mushrooms, which will not be very interesting in this recipe.

Allowing one breast per person, remove the breasts from the pheasants, keeping their skins intact. The birds required are first season's; no old lags allowed. Hens are reckoned to be less dry and of finer flavour; this is a counsel of perfection, especially as the poaching will be a gentle medium. The legs are not needed for this recipe; a game pie for them. Having removed the legs and breasts, put the carcases in a good chicken stock and cook them.

Soak the morels (three per person) in cold water for two hours. Do not throw away the water, rather add it to the stock. This, which should now be quite rich, is the poaching medium. Take a pan, place the breasts and the morels therein and cover with the stock. Bring to simmering point, put a cover on, and cook very gently for 15 to 30 minutes. The time will depend on the age of the birds.

When satisfied that they are tender, remove the pheasant and the fungi and reserve in a warm spot. Start to reduce the juice vigorously; add 2fl oz / 60ml of double cream per person and continue to reduce until the sauce is glossy. Do not season until this point. If done before the reduction is begun there may be too much salt.

Skin and slice the breasts, pop the morels on top and pour over the sauce.

Meat dishes

SAUSAGES

We were first provoked into making sausages by reading Richard Olney's instructions for some rabbit in *Simple French Food* (1981). Although such things have barely entered the realms of high cooking, the fashion for packing flesh into parcels has ever been there and has experienced a revival with smart chefs doing fish sausages and the like. I am not sure that there is much difference between wrapping your mixture in tubular sausage casings and wrapping them in caul to make a faggot. In neither case does the outer skin contribute much to the flavour, merely tidying up the stuffing and protecting it from the cooking medium. In like manner, a boned quail wrapped in caul will be a more delicate affair, because protected, than the same bird roasted naked. Making sausages of this nature is quite another matter from the cured and dried salamis that more truly reflect the derivation of the word from the Latin *salsus,* salt.

For sausages, you need a piping bag, a broad nozzle, some sausage casing and a food processor or mincer. We have never owned a sausage-filling attachment such as is sold as part of a domestic mincer and find that the task is not impossible by hand. As the attachment depends on the ingredients being minced on their way to the casing, it is not wholly satisfactory if you want texture. The casings that we buy from a butcher who makes his own bangers do not require a preliminary soak. However, they are fairly evil-smelling, from the preservative, and handling with rubber gloves is not a bad idea. If you find them inextricable in the first instance, they can be soaked in vinegar and water and straightened out by putting on to the tap and filling with water.

Working with a length of about three feet, you slide the bulk of the casing over the nozzle of the piping bag containing the meat filling. Squeeze hard yet with calm, extruding the filling into skin, paying it out as you go. If the work is roughly handled, the skin will split. A certain amount of jiggling about is needed to exclude air bubbles. The whole process reminds me of rethreading a pyjama cord. On good days, it works like a dream; at other times, there can be two of you getting very bad-tempered and frustrated indeed. When you have filled the length of casing and got rid of pockets of air, the ends may be tied up and the whole may be twisted into little sausages, each no more than three inches long. Some suggest using a large funnel (rescued from the garage?). I found this tool worse than useless, incapable of exerting enough pressure on the filling, the casing constantly slipping off.

That the process can be one of pleasure and excitement is demonstrated by an account of turning pigs into meals that was contributed to *Twelve Times* by our neighbour, Gay Lange.

From the flesh of the neck, blade, spareribs, belly and fat, all marinated over one night in brine, we made sausages. These were undoubtedly our success, although the making of them caused more exhaustion and time than anything else. For future reference we know that a domestic electric mincer attachment to a food mixer is insufficient to cope with eighteen pounds of raw pork meat and fat; not, that is to say, if the operator is to keep his or her sanity . . . However, once the mincing was over, the fun of seasoning began. We added just one loaf of good white bread to the 18lb of meat and then forget recipes and relied on taste and imagination. Soaked dried apples, chestnuts, juniper berries, green peppercorns, moistening with vodka, port, elderberry wine – the difficulty was to restrict ourselves to three different combinations for three kinds of sausages.

Filling sausage casings, so lightly dismissed by me, can be avoided by any who know themselves to attract disaster. Use caul instead. Such an envelope will not stand up so robustly to the preliminary boiling that is given to sausages, but it is not impossible.

As it was Richard Olney that drew us into sausages, it was his recipe that we used as a base for our own mixtures, though omitting the thickening from blood that he counsels. One of the dangers, particularly if the meat is light in flavour, comes from grinding it too finely. There must be some chopped texture to preserve taste and interest. Anything can be tried; it is an excellent way of using scraps of game. The most enjoyable were with legs of grouse, using the breasts for a main course. Similarly, pheasant or hare may be tried.

8oz / 225g raw game flesh, off the bone, skinned	1½oz / 40g crumb of home made white bread (not steam baked)
4oz / 125g fat salt belly pork	4fl oz / 120ml milk
4oz / 125g lean pork or veal	3oz / 75g onions
2 eggs	Parsley, thyme, marjoram *or* 3 juniper berries

Cook the milk and the bread together to make a *panada*, cool. Chop the onion finely and sweat in a little butter without colouring, cool. Chop or grind your meats. Grind some in the mincer or processor, but not excessively, and chop some very well by hand. Coarse texture can make it more difficult to fill the casing. Chop the herbs or crush the berries. Combine everything in a bowl, adding the eggs and generous seasoning. Fill the casing. This amount is about right for a three-foot length. Tie up the sausages and cut them apart before poaching in barely simmering water for ten minutes. Refresh them in cold water, drain and dry. Refrigerate. For the final cooking, they can be grilled or fried.

No one can disguise that sausages, even the worst manufactured items, are extremely rich. The home-made versions should be treated with care. The act of boiling does reduce some of their impact. With the very best pure pork sausages made by genuine people, for instance Heal Farm in north Devon, a light poaching helps in the same way. A side dish of red cabbage, cooked with vinegar, apple, onion and sugar, helps lighten the load still further.

LAMB TOURNEDOS

This is one of the most expensive ways of dealing with lamb. It is also one of the best. Although the preparatory butchery is tedious, the cooking is extremely simple and rapid. It is therefore possible to cook this for a dinner party with minimum absence from the table.

Order a long loin of lamb from the butcher. This will be one side of the backbone, running from the best end of neck through to chump chops above the leg. The nut of meat and the fillet from this joint need to be detached by cutting through the connective tissue from the under-side, removing any bones at the chump end and peeling the meat from the top skin with your fingers and a little help from a sharp knife. The tiny fillet, which rests on a layer of fat on the underside of the loin, can be taken out with the fingers prior to this.

The rest of the joint may then be used elsewhere. We strip the meat off the flank and make 'lamb-burgers' or spiced meat balls after mincing the trimmings, rid of most but not all their fat, and mixing them with cumin and cardamom, served with a strong tomato sauce and yoghurt for staff lunch.

After the nut of meat is thus removed, it needs to be trimmed of any remaining fat and skin. This is a delicate operation undertaken with a small and very sharp knife, removing the thin tissue or membrane surrounding the flesh without taking the meat at the same time. Once trimmed, cut the meat into tournedos. Each of these should weigh 2–3oz / 50–80g and be not more than 1½in / 3cm thick. A tournedos may consist of two or even three pieces of meat, each showing the end grain to the heat, so incorporating the fillet or joining together two pieces from the small end of the loin. The constituents coalesce to a degree in the cooking. Wrap each tournedos with a piece of bacon, trimmed of rind and bone, secured with a cocktail stick. Use streaky bacon, of a cure that is not too salty.

Season the tournedos with pepper and a little salt. Heat a heavy pan with oil and butter until nearly smoking and sear them on both sides very briefly before placing, uncovered, in a preheated oven 220°c / 425°F / gas mark 7, for four minutes. They should be pink.

This is really expensive meat, especially at the beginning of the lamb season. However, it makes a change from the almost invariable rack of lamb and produces a more succulent piece of meat. A length of loin will not do many more than four or five people. But be comforted that people cannot eat too much meat cooked in this way. 6oz / 170g is more than enough and a scant 5oz / 140g will not be found meagre.

The dish looks stark on the plate and responds well to a good vegetable accompaniment – which also avoids problems caused by too fine assessment of quantities. Serve a simple gravy made by deglazing the pan with red wine, adding a spoonful of redcurrant or apple and mint jelly, and mounting with a little butter. Often *dauphinois* potatoes are a good choice with tournedos and we have sometimes served them with tartlets filled with a strong tomato mixture or with an artichoke purée. Another thing to do is three vegetable purées; peas are very good, celeriac another, and broccoli with walnut oil a third. A gravy then becomes essential. Our most common accompaniments, however, are either a *peperonata*, where the juice from the vegetables affords the meat some of its benefits, or stuffed courgette flowers and the first of the young courgettes tossed in butter.

The important things to ensure are that your tournedos are the right size, that they are nicely, but not excessively, browned on entry to the oven and that they are not overcooked. Like most pieces of meat, they will benefit from a minute or two resting in a warm place after they have been brought from the oven.

DARTMOUTH PIE, 1978

Dartmouth Pie
Mince two pounds of mutton, from which all the fat has been cut away,
and add it to one pound of finely shredded beef suet, one pound of well-
washed currants, four ounces of sugar, and a little salt and nutmeg.
Make a paste by boiling two ounces of butter with four ounces of beef
suet, and working it into eight ounces of flour. Cover the mixture with
this paste, and bake for an hour and a half.
   Cassell's Dictionary of Cookery (1896)
This is plainly an old recipe and name, for there is an earlier version by
John Nott, in his *Cook's Dictionary* of 1726.

A Devonshire Squab-Pye
Make a good crust, cover the dish all over, put at the bottom a layer of
sliced pippins, strew over them some sugar, then a layer of mutton-
stakes, cut from the loin, well seasoned with pepper and salt, then
another layer of pippins; peel some onions and slice them thin, lay a
layer all over the apples, then a layer of mutton, then pippins and
onions; pour in a pint of water, so close your pye and bake it.
   Hannah Glasse, *The Art of Cookery* (1747)

To make Mince Pyes without Meat
Take a pound of apples, a pound and a half of suet, half a pound of
raisins stoned, half a pound of prunes stoned; chop all these very fine,
and add to them half a pound of sugar, two drachms of mace, a nutmeg,
and a little salt; put to it half a pint of white wine, some brandy, and
currant jelly; put in the currants when you make it up.
   The Family Cookery Book (1812)

In his entry for Devonshire in *Kettner's Book of the Table* (1877), E. S.
Dallas remarked that the county was famed for its butter, not so good as
Breton, Norman or that from Ostend, but still the best in Britain, its
clotted cream, its cider and its pie, 'also called Squab Pie, ... made of
Devonshire apples and of Devonshire (that is Dartmoor) mutton, or else
of pork'. In Hannah Glasse, a pork and apple pie goes by the name of
Cheshire, though for Richard Bradley (1736), the name implied a pork
and potato pie. The Cornish also produced this Squab Pie and Dallas
observes that as often as not pork was the meat used. Indeed, Francatelli
(1861) thought Devonshire Pie consisted of pork, bacon and apples.

The combination of mutton and apple is reputed somewhat dubiously to mirror the taste of squabs, that is, fledgling pigeons or other young birds. Perhaps the name refers to the shape of the pie: another meaning of squab, in use by the seventeenth century, was cushion. Charles Carter (1730) has a note on Mutton Squab Pie, not giving it a geographical name, which includes mutton cutlets, apples and onions, beef suet, raising and nutmeg. His sweet lamb pie includes a greater number of spices, citrus peel and dates.

Later versions of these dishes are slightly different. Jane Grigson's (*Good Things, 1971*) is a mutton and apple pie, with prunes and spices taken in from a mincemeat recipe. Theodora Fitzgibbon (*A Taste of the West Country, 1972*) considers Devon Pork Pie, made with apples, onions or leeks to be the same as Dartmouth Pie and, if made with veal or lamb, to be Squab Pie. It is difficult to unravel the course of these instructions from century to century. There is no local tradition that I have ever heard tell. When we came to make our own Dartmouth Pie, therefore, we felt uninhibited in mingling ingredients from one stream or another. The principle that guided us was the combination of mutton with fruit and spices that might thus be reminiscent of a mincemeat recipe such as the Cassell's; at the same time that it should remind us of mutton and apple along the Squab Pie lines. However, it became innocent of apple thus having less connection with this stream than at first intended. It makes a good winter dish.

2 teaspoons black peppercorns	5oz / 140g dried prunes
1 teaspoon blade mace	4oz / 110g raisins
1 teaspoon whole allspice	Rind and juice of an orange
2 inches cinnamon stick	(preferably Seville)
2 teaspoons coriander	1lb / 450g onions
2lb / 900g trimmed leg of	10fl oz / 300ml beef stock
mutton	1 tablespoon flour
5oz / 140g dried apricots	Salt and dripping

The reason we first started to look at the pie recipes was because we were able to get mutton. No longer is it the lean, strongly flavoured meat of four year old ewes that was once available, but it is sufficiently grown to be different from lamb. Take the meat off the bone, rid it of all fat and cut it into cubes 1in / 2.5cm square.

Grind the spices together. Season the meat with salt and brown it in a heavy pan with dripping. Add the spices and fry some more. Slice the onions finely and add them to the meat. Continue frying, add the flour to make a *roux*, add the stock and simmer briefly to amalgamate.

Put the dried fruit into a good casserole. There is no need to soak it, but stoned prunes are preferable to unstoned. Add the contents of the frying pan and bring the whole to the boil. Add the grated rind and the juice of an orange. If a Seville is possible, so much the better. We keep some of them in the freezer from January to January for such an eventuality. Check the seasoning, cover and cook in a cool oven (130°C / 250°F / gas mark ½) for about an hour and a half until the meat is tender.

It is best if the pie filling is pre-cooked in this way. The spices then have a chance to be absorbed and matured before reheating the following day. Put the filling in a pie dish, cover with a crust (short or flaky, although Devonians would have used short) and bake in a hot oven until the filling is thoroughly heated and the crust is browned. If the former looks like taking longer than the latter, and it probably will unless you have heated the pie filling beforehand, protect the crust with foil.

JULIENNE OF VEAL WITH VEGETABLES AND SORREL

1lb / 450g fillet of veal (or other tender joint)	1oz / 25g French beans
2oz / 50g onions	1oz / 25g sorrel
2oz / 50g carrots	8fl oz / 240ml double cream
1oz / 25g celery or celeriac	3½oz / 90g butter
1oz / 25g courgettes	Salt, pepper and lemon juice

Trim the veal of any skin, gristle or fat and cut it into strips about 1½in / 3cm long and the width of a pencil, as if for beef Stroganoff. Prepare and cut the vegetables into smaller strips. Wash and strip the sorrel and shred it. Sweat the hard vegetables with some seasoning in 1½oz / 40g of butter for about five minutes in a covered pan over a low flame. Add the courgettes and beans and leave for a further three minutes.

Season the veal with salt, pepper and lemon juice. Throw it into a wide pan in which you have melted the rest of the butter and turn the heat to high. Fry briefly and add the vegetables; mix and add the double cream and the sorrel. Bring back to the boil, shake together then lift the meat and vegetables on to a serving dish to keep warm while the cream is reduced in the pan to a coating consistency. Taste and adjust seasoning. The process is very quick. The aim is to get the richness of the cream and butter well overlaid with the sharpness of the sorrel. If too much lemon juice is added, the sorrel vanishes beneath its strength.

CALF'S LIVER WITH CAPERS

The usual method of dealing with calf's liver is to slice it thinly and fry it lightly. This may be a reaction to its cost: treat it like a delicacy. But the more robust mode of cutting it as a steak, often found in French kitchens, offers greater succulence and flavour. Braising such a joint seems *lèse majesté*, but a recipe with which we have had great success involves just that. The result was liver the palest pink throughout, moist and as delicate a flavour as could be hoped for. The original is given by Jacques Médecin in *Cuisine Niçoise* (1983) where he describes a dish sufficient for twenty people. Small likelihood this will be performed, so we have adapted it for smaller groups. This serves eight.

1 piece of calf's liver, about 2lbs / 900g weight
1 large onion
1 clove garlic
2 beefsteak or Marmande tomatoes

5fl oz / 150ml chicken or veal stock
Small jar of capers
Thyme, marjoram and parsley
Salt, pepper and oil

Slice the onion and garlic thinly. Sweat them in oil in a large heavy casserole with the herbs. Skin and trim the liver. Season it and place on top of the sweated vegetables. I have not larded the liver, a practice usual with large pieces, yet it did not dry out. Cover closely and put in a hot oven (200°C / 400°F / gas mark 6). It will take about twenty-five minutes; turn it half way through.

In the meantime, peel, deseed and chop the tomatoes and simmer them in stock. It is useful to have a strong-flavoured stock. Check the seasoning. When the liver is done, remove it to a warm place from the casserole and pour the tomatoes on to the onions. Reduce by boiling and taste for a strongish sauce. Slice the liver on to a serving dish; strew with drained capers and pour over the sauce.

Richard Bradley (1736) advises a roast liver, stuffed with suet, breadcrumbs, herbs and currants and sent up with melted butter and lemon juice, garnished with slices of lemon and pickled barberries – the fruit of the berberis. The accompaniment would have the same effect as the capers in the Provençal dish.

Ice creams and sorbets

HONEY AND CARDAMOM ICE CREAM

A particularly successful use of this ice cream has been in a cake made of layers of meringue separated by honey and cardamom, coffee, and caramel ice creams. Another is to make brown sugar meringues in the shape of nests, fill with this ice and serve with clotted cream.

½pt / 300ml milk
5fl oz / 150ml honey
2 egg yolks

5fl oz / 150ml double cream
1 teaspoon cardamom pods

Grind or crush the cardamom pods, without hulling them. Mix them with the milk, bring to the boil and infuse for twenty minutes. Strain through a muslin. Add the honey to the milk and bring back to the boil.

Whisk the yolks together with the cream. Pour on the milk as it rises to the boil. Whisk together, cook in a water bath or double boiler until it coats the back of a spoon and strain through a fine sieve. Cool then freeze in a machine or in a container in the freezer, in which case stir with a fork at intervals to stop crystallisation.

MANGO AND PASSION-FRUIT ICE CREAM

Mangoes and passion fruit! Who would have thought, even five years ago, that they would now be part of the *lingua franca* of the English kitchen? The advantage of the tropical fruits is their availability at times when the domestic product, apples apart, is scanty. They bring a perfume into a meal that may sometimes sit uneasily with western accompaniments but nevertheless add new colours to our palette.

Take a very ripe mango. This may mean buying it and waiting for it to ripen on the kitchen shelf. Take four passion fruit. Peel the mango and slice the flesh off the stone. Halve the passion fruit, scoop out the seeds and rub them hard through a sieve. Add the result to the mango and weigh. Take 1oz / 25g of caster sugar to each 2oz / 50g of fruit. Blend to a purée. Sharpen the flavour with lemon juice. Stir in 1fl oz / 30ml of double cream to each 2oz / 50g of fruit and freeze.

STRAWBERRY AND ROSE PETAL ICE CREAM

1lb / 450g ripe strawberries   Juice of half a lemon
1 large rose   10fl oz / 300ml double cream
8oz / 225g caster sugar

Blend the strawberries with the sugar, lemon juice and rose petals in an electric blender. Add the cream and freeze. If made without an ice cream machine, remove from the freezer and stir on two occasions during the freezing.

We have on occasion combined this with a pineapple ice cream in a *bombe* mould.

ROSE PETAL AND SAUTERNES SORBET

7fl oz / 200ml Sauternes   5fl oz / 150 ml water
7fl oz / 200ml stock syrup   4 to 6 fragrant red roses
  (made to the proportions of   Juice of a lemon
  7oz / 200g of sugar to 7fl oz /
  200ml of water)

Pick off the rose petals and blend them with the water. Strain the fluid, pressing well, and reserve. Add it to the rest of the ingredients and freeze. If without an ice cream machine, stir at intervals with a fork to inhibit crystallisation.

This is very refreshing. The quality of the wine does matter. If you cannot afford a decent Sauternes, use Muscat.

Cold desserts

CUSTARD-APPLE MOUSSE

The mixture of flavours in a custard apple is mysterious – strawberries and cream, bananas, pineapple – all have their place. A mousse made with them is tantalising.

10oz / 275g custard apple purée (raw)
Juice of half a lemon
2 sheets of gelatine
3oz / 75g caster sugar
5fl oz / 150ml double cream
2 whites of egg

Soak the gelatine in a little cold water and dissolve in the slightly warmed juice of lemon. Mix the puréed fruit and the sugar and add the gelatine and lemon juice. Lightly whip the double cream and fold into the cooled fruit mixture. Stiffly whip the whites and fold them in. It is as well to keep all ingredients cool and to execute the foldings just as the gelatine is starting to take hold. This will give maximum lightness.

FRUIT SALAD

In the stuffiest of grand hotels where food is badly cooked, boring and heavy, one thing to fall back on is fruit salad. It may be at least fresh and uncomplicated, though pale-faced. Apples, pears, oranges, bananas, grapes, a dash of cherry red, the crunch of the apples compensating for the presence of tinned peaches. Now, the advent of tropical fruits in most greengrocers can change that. A salad of a heady perfume; dark and luscious hues; what follows is no recipe, merely a guide.

The syrup is made with 2oz / 50g sugar to 5fl oz / 150ml water, dissolved, brought to the boil and two lengths of lemon peel pared into it. No alcohol is needed.

Fruits: blackberries, black currants, red currants, plums, pears, peaches, nectarines, raspberries, cherries, bananas, mango, paw paw and watermelon.

The tropical fruits need to be ripe to give off their best fragrance. The currants, berries and watermelon lend a glorious colour. The absence of apples and oranges is to be supported. The coincidence of this particular set of fruits does not last long. Try it when it does.

MELON, REDCURRANTS AND CASSIS

A pleasant summer dish.

1 Charentais melon	3fl oz / 90ml water
2 punnets redcurrants	2fl oz / 60ml *cassis*
4oz / 110g white sugar	Juice of half a lemon

Make a syrup of the sugar and water; take off the heat; add the *cassis*; add the redcurrants. Let this cool fully. Season with the lemon juice. Cut the melon into slices; peel these and cut further into thin chunks. Mix

LAVENDER CUSTARD

With most floral recipes, if the taste is too strong, some back flavours begin to rear up, destroying the pleasure which is drawn from the perfume and the hint of the summer arbour. So with lavender, there is a bitterness and resinous quality if you overstep the mark. But this custard has some quality. Lavender is not a bloom used much in cooking. There is the Alice Waters recipe for honey ice cream with lavender from modern California, and Frances Bissell includes some interesting uses in *A Cook's Calendar* (1985).

Infuse 5 lavender flower heads in 1pt / 60 ml milk for half an hour. Use the hot milk to make a custard with 1oz / 25g caster sugar, four yolks and one whole egg. Pour the scalded milk and sugar on to the beaten eggs, and strain into a dish. Cook the custard until set in a water bath, with a lid to the custard pot, in a slow oven (130°C / 250°F / gas mark ½). To add to the luxury, you can mix cream and milk together though this always separates into two layers in the cooking.

APPLES AND PEARS IN A SAUTERNES JELLY

A simple recipe that makes a little food go a long way. Jellies are delicious, yet outside households with children they get short shrift. Certainly they are never the most popular item on a restaurant menu. Perhaps there is a latent fear of the rock-set commercial jelly founded on artificial flavouring. Alternatively, people eat so much jelly at home, they never wish to see one when out – nor would you order cornflakes, banana and cream. But think of peaches in a pink jelly; soft fruits in a maraschino jelly; pears in a claret and port jelly; kirsch jelly. The list could be extended. With leaf gelatine (safer than powdered) such flavours are easily achievable.

Apples and pears

8oz / 225g sugar

10fl oz / 300ml water

10fl oz / 300ml Sauternes

5 sheets of gelatine

Take as many apples and pears, peeled, cored and sliced, as you need, approximately one fruit per person. Poach them very lightly in a syrup of 8oz / 225g sugar, 10fl oz / 300ml water and 10fl oz / 30ml Sauternes or other sweet wine.

Soak the gelatine in cold water. Remove the fruit with a slotted spoon, measure 1pt / 600ml of liquid and add the gelatine to this, stirring until dissolved. Check the taste; add lemon juice if desired.

Pour about half the liquid into glasses or a larger bowl. Put in the refrigerator. Add the fruit when setting has commenced, then pour on the remainder of the liquid. This amount of gelatine will give a reasonably firm jelly. Any syrup left over can be used for stewing fruit on subsequent days.

ROSE PETALS

Culinary use of flowers has come back into fashion, though more encountered in the private home than in the restaurant. There is no better guide than Claire Clifton's *Edible Flowers* (1983). We have been fortunate in having wonderfully fragrant blooms given to us by an owner of a deep red climbing rose. Its season is extended, in a good year, so that we can incorporate dishes based on its perfume from Whitsun to Michaelmas. An old-fashioned damask rose is better than many of the newer varieties.

The first thing to do is to crystallise some of the petals for decoration. Primroses and violets get the same treatment earlier in the year. Brush them with a little gum arabic (available from chemists) dissolved in alcohol (vodka); sprinkle them with caster sugar; leave them to dry on a rack in a warm place. Preserve them in an airtight box.

There are several ways in which the flower heads can be used directly. Rhubarb and rose petal jam, one flower head to each pound of rhubarb; chopped finely into a Chantilly cream to serve with soft fruit; as a sorbet, with or without some Sauternes; with strawberries in an ice cream; in a *bavarois* with almonds; in a variety of *bombe* moulds, the most elaborate of which was an outer layer of loganberry ice cream, the next of raspberry, and the core a rose petal ice with cherries that we had soaked in kirsch embedded in it. This need not be a *bombe*, layers in a loaf tin would do as well. The rose should be very smelly.

ALMOND AND ROSE PETAL CREAM

Almond cream

2 yolks of egg
3 bitter almonds
2oz / 50g sugar

5fl oz / 150ml milk
5fl oz / 150ml double cream
2 sheets of gelatine

Grind the almonds in a coffee grinder or pestle and mortar with a little sugar. Add to the milk and infuse them over the heat for five minutes. Strain the milk into a double boiler and make into a custard with the yolks and the rest of the sugar. Soak the sheets of gelatine in cold water, squeeze them dry and add to the custard off the heat. Stir to dissolve and allow to cool. Whip the double cream lightly and fold into the almond cream.

Rose petal cream

3 large red roses
2 yolks of egg
2oz / 50g sugar
5fl oz / 150ml milk

5fl oz / 150ml double cream
2 sheets of gelatine
Juice of ¼ of a lemon

Make a custard with the yolks, the sugar and the milk. Add the softened gelatine off the heat and stir to dissolve. Pick the rose petals and put them in the blender with the lemon juice. Whizz. Add the custard and whizz until smooth. Lightly whip the cream and fold into the custard.

Take an oiled jelly mould and put alternate layers of the creams. Leave to set before serving.

ROSE PETAL CHANTILLY CREAM

2 large red roses
3fl oz / 90ml single cream
Juice of ½ a small lemon

1 tablespoon vanilla sugar
8fl oz / 240ml double cream

Pick the petals off the flowers heads and put in a blender with single cream. Whizz until smooth. Keep in the refrigerator.

Over a bowl of ice, if you want extra volume, combine all the ingredients and whisk until thick.

PRUNES AND RASPBERRIES WITH DESSERT WINE AND AN ALMOND CREAM

Prunes and raspberries

1lb / 450g Californian jumbo
   prunes
Half a bottle of Sauternes

1 tablespoon of redcurrant jelly
8oz / 225g raspberries

Soak the prunes in the wine overnight or through the day. Add the redcurrant jelly and barely simmer for some twenty minutes until tender. Remove the prunes and reduce the syrup, tasting for sweetness. Pour over the prunes. Add the raspberries while everything is still warm to release some of their fragrance. This is a fair way of using the end-of-season raspberries that may lack sufficient fruit to be eaten on their own.

Almond cream

This is similar in most respects to the almond cream used in conjunction with the rose petal cream; its bland taste is a good accompaniment to the stewed fruit.

1oz / 25g whole almonds, peeled
   and blanched
6 bitter almonds, unpeeled
10fl oz / 300ml milk

4 yolks of egg
2oz / 50g caster sugar
4 sheets leaf gelatine
10fl oz / 300ml double cream

Chop the almonds finely. Soak the gelatine. Heat the milk and pour on to the creamed yolks and sugar. Return to the heat with the chopped almonds; use a double boiler. Make a custard that coats the back of the spoon. Strain this through a medium sieve. Add the drained gelatine and stir to dissolve; leave to cool. Whip the double cream lightly and fold into the mixture. Place in an oiled mould.

WALNUT OR HAZELNUT SHORT BISCUITS

Not a difficult mixture to make successfully, although much easier if a food processor is available. They can be used in a variety of ways at the dessert; one of the simplest yet most effective is to sandwich them with clotted cream and strawberries.

7oz / 200g unsalted butter   1 egg
5oz / 140g caster sugar   8oz / 225g self-raising flour
3oz / 75g walnuts or peeled
   hazelnuts

This can be put in the food processor, only stopping to peel the hazelnuts (by roasting them and rubbing them in a cloth) and to soften, not melt, the butter. A few short bursts and it can be brought together and removed. Otherwise, chop the nuts fine, soften the butter, beat the egg, sift the flour and sugar together and combine the ingredients. There is a danger of the mixture becoming too short if it is worked too much. Bring the paste into a roll wrapped in foil or greaseproof (as if it were a herb butter) and leave in the refrigerator to chill.

Grease an oven tray to prepare your oven for moderate heat (180°C / 350°F / gas mark 4). Cut ⅛in / 3mm rounds off the roll and lay them on the tray. Bake for ten minutes, until they have taken colour. They will be soft at first but will harden as they cool. Preserve in an airtight box.

BRANDY SNAPS WITH LEMON SYLLABUB

I have always been surprised at how popular these biscuits are, no matter what their filling. Normally we make a citrus cream of some sort, such as this syllabub. The brandy snaps are cooked according to the instructions in Hanneman's *Pâtisserie*, a professional handbook. It is a reliable, and slightly simpler, method.

4½oz / 125g soft butter   4oz / 110g golden syrup
8oz / 225g caster sugar   1 level teaspoon ground ginger
4oz / 110g plain flour

Have all the ingredients at room temperature and mix to a smooth paste. There is no need to warm the butter, sugar and syrup as in other recipes. Accurate measurement is wise. The paste will resemble marzipan in handling.

Preheat the oven to 170°C / 325°F / gas mark 3 and use well-greased trays. Roll the mixture into small balls and press them slightly flat with the palm of the hand on to the trays. Use small trays and do only a few at a time. Bake for about five minutes until golden brown. Roll each snap, immediately upon exit from the oven, on a wooden spoon handle (for a cigarette) or a horn mould (for a cone). Careful watching and timing is necessary to prevent burning.

Hanneman recommends that you use soft flour, as used in cakes, not the hard wheat bread flour that is increasingly popular. Made with a very hard flour, they sometimes do not spread on the trays. General purpose plain flour found in the supermarkets works very well.

Lemon wine syllabub

This is a very simple cream that goes well with the snaps. It can be piped or spooned into them, or can be served as a dip. Made with wine, it is less assertive than when sherry and brandy are used, as in many syllabubs.

10fl oz / 300ml double cream	Rind and juice of half a lemon
2fl oz / 60ml sweet white wine	1oz / 25g caster sugar

Grate the rind of a lemon. Combine all the ingredients, when they are as cold as possible, and whip them lightly. Check for taste after the rind has had a chance to infuse.

CHOCOLATE *ROULADE* WITH A GINGER CREAM

This *roulade* recipe came to us first from a girl who had been on a London Cordon Bleu course. It is not, however, in Constance Spry. Nonetheless, the flourless, fatless sponge, which bears much resemblance to the recipe for the hot chocolate soufflé given below, has gained in popularity. *Roulades* are fast becoming hackneyed in English catering cookery.

3oz / 75g caster sugar	3oz / 75g plain chocolate
3 eggs	2fl oz / 60ml brandy

Melt the chocolate with the brandy in a *bain-marie*. Beat it smooth and let cool. Separate the eggs and put the yolks with the sugar. Beat them until pale and stir in the chocolate. Beat the whites to soft peaks and fold in to the rest of the ingredients.

Bake this in a shallow tray lined with clingfilm. The mixture should be about ½in / 1.5cm thick. Bake for 15 minutes (190°C / 375°F / gas mark 5). It will rise and then, alas, fall. Leave it to cool in the tray. It can be left quite a time without coming to any harm.

Turn it out of the tray on to a sheet of foil spread on the kitchen table. Peel away the clingfilm. Smooth the filling over the sponge and use the foil to aid your rolling into a Swiss roll shape. This, of course, is the tricky bit. It may crack as it rolls but such problems are not irremediable. It can be patched or covered with more cream. Take care not to drop the completed roll in transferring it to a dish.

The filling here specified is ½pt / 300ml whipped double cream mixed with a tablespoonful of chopped stem ginger and some of its syrup. The combination is pleasant.

CHOCOLATE ALMOND MERINGUE CAKE

There are two processes involved: the meringue and the chocolate.

Meringue

3 whites of egg	3oz / 75g ground almonds
3oz / 75g caster sugar	3oz / 75g caster sugar

Prepare three baking trays. Lay out sheets of siliconised paper or line them with foil sprinkled with flour and mark out three rings (using a 7in / 18cm flan ring as a guide).

Whip the whites very stiffly and beat in the first batch of sugar. Mix the almonds and the second batch together and fold them into the meringue when it has been sufficiently beaten. Spread the meringue in the ring shapes. A piping bag is convenient.

Cook the meringue: either a short burst of low gas for fifteen minutes, then left in the oven with the pilot light for the afternoon or the night; or an hour at gas 1; or in the cool oven of a solid-fuel cooker until dried out; or at 140°C / 275°F for an hour in an electric oven. Take care when removing it from the foil. Put it in a sealed box, or a foil wrapping, until you need it.

Chocolate cream

6oz / 160g plain chocolate	1 flat dessertspoonful instant
1½oz / 40g unsalted butter	coffee
1½fl oz / 45ml water	1½fl oz / 45ml brandy
	6fl oz / 180ml double cream

Melt the chocolate with the unsalted butter and water in a *bain-marie*. Beat to ensure smoothness and add the instant coffee. Add the brandy when it has cooled somewhat. Whip the cream lightly and stir in the chocolate and brandy. Cool completely, but not so much as to solidify.

Assembly

Layer the meringues with the chocolate cream. The taste may be enriched by melting 4oz / 110g of plain chocolate in a little water and spreading on the top sides of the meringues. This also protects the meringues from too great absorption of liquid from the cream. The constructed cake may seem a little untidy. Trim the edges with a sharp knife and finish off by trowelling smooth any cream bulging out of the edges with the blade of a palette knife. If you have any meringue crumbs from the trimming, they can be crushed and spread on the now sticky sides of the cake.

ICED MOCHA MOUSSE

This is a recipe that was suggested to us by a kind subscriber who had used it with success from *Good Housekeeping* magazine. It is always interesting observing the disparate origins of the dishes one cooks. There is so great an output of recipes, in books, magazines and so forth, that some at least must be winners. The quantities seem to give a good mocha flavour without imbalance.

4oz / 110g plain chocolate	4oz / 110g sugar
1½oz / 40g ground coffee	Whites of 2 eggs
5fl oz / 150ml milk	8fl oz / 240ml double cream

Infuse the coffee in the milk on top of the stove. Squeeze out through a muslin to obtain every last drop. Then melt the chocolate in the milk, beating to ensure smoothness.

Make an Italian meringue with the whites by putting them in a large bowl set over a pan of hot, not boiling, water. Whisk them until stiff, adding the sugar. Remove them from the heat and whisk for another three minutes. Whip the cream lightly in another bowl.

Make the final combination when all the ingredients have cooled. Fold the ingredients together and pour into a clingfilm-lined mould, for example a loaf tin. Place in the freezer. It will not freeze very hard.

This can be served with a chocolate sauce and a short biscuit made with walnuts. It has the advantage of requiring only egg whites. As there is often a surplus after making *hollandaise* or mayonnaise or thickening *liaisons* it makes a change from the inevitable meringue nests or meringue cake.

CHARLOTTE LOUISE

Another extremely extravagant and rich chocolate dessert, the quantities of which could well be halved.

8oz / 225g plain chocolate	Juice and zest of 1 large orange
2oz / 50g butter	1fl oz / 30ml orange Curaçao
10fl oz / 300ml double cream	Sponge fingers

Soak your sponge fingers, sufficient for the charlotte mould (which may be a straight-sided 5in / 12.5cm china soufflé dish), in the Curaçao and line the dish, bottom and sides.

Melt the butter and chocolate together over hot water, beating until smooth. Add the grated zests of the oranges and the juice. Leave to cool. Lightly whisk the double cream until stiff and fold together with the chocolate. Put into the charlotte mould and leave for two days before slicing.

This needs an uncomplicated sauce to help it along; at its simplest, a vanilla custard.

GOOSEBERRY TART

1½lbs / 675g gooseberries	Sweet pastry or puff pastry
2oz / 50g unsalted butter	5fl oz / 150ml water
3 eggs	4oz / 110g sugar
2oz / 50g sugar	4 heads of elderflowers

Roll out the pastry thinly and line a 10in / 25cm flan case, bake it blind. Make a purée of the gooseberries: cook them, after washing, with the butter, then whizz and sieve them. There is no need to add more water. Add about two ounces of sugar to each pint of purée. More can be added, depending on the type and season of the berries, but the butter and the eggs will soften their acidity. Let the purée cool and add three eggs (per 1pt / 600ml), beating the while. Make a syrup with the water and sugar, let it cool and marinate the elderflowers for an hour before straining off. Fill the flan with the purée. Cook in a moderate oven (190°C / 375°F / gas mark 5) for about half an hour until it is set. When removed from the oven, brush on the syrup. The heat of the tart will evaporate the water and leave you with a slight and perfumed glaze.

This is but a variation on a method standard in the eighteenth century. Jane Grigson, in *Good Things* (1971), adapts a Hannah Glasse recipe for gooseberry cream that is virtually identical. The immediate inspiration for this, however, was *The Family Cookery Book*, printed at Coventry in 1812. It contains three items that bear upon our instructions. The first is a pudding, with 3 eggs, a pint of purée, 1½ ounces of butter, sweet crumbs and sugar baked in a flan. The second is a pint of purée, 2 ounces of butter, a quarter of cream, 4 yolks and 3 whites, sugar and lemon peel or orange flower water. Again, it is baked with puff paste. The third is for gooseberry cheesecakes. Equal quantities of purée and sugar (8 ounces), sweet crumbs, lemon rind, 4 whole eggs and 6 ounces of butter are put into a puff case.

GOOSEBERRIES WITH A HONEY AND SAFFRON CREAM

This was a recipe that Joyce Molyneux gave to Jane Grigson for her *Observer Guide to British Cookery* (1984). The combination of honey and saffron is delectable. It can be done with rhubarb too.

6oz / 160g gooseberries	3oz / 75g honey
2oz / 50g sugar	8 yolks
1 pint / 600ml single cream	1 packet (a good pinch) saffron

Cook the gooseberries in the bottom of a buttered dish – merely sprinkle them with sugar and bake in a cool oven for fifteen minutes.

Pound the saffron threads in the mortar to extract their goodness. Make a custard of the honey, cream and egg yolks in a double boiler, adding the saffron. Cook it until it coats the back of a spoon. Pour the custard on to the gooseberries and place the dish in a shallow *bain-marie*. Put this into a cool oven and bake until just set (140°C / 275 / gas mark 1 for 25 minutes).

Jane Grigson makes the point that baking the gooseberries will toughen their skins and suggests cooking them on top of the stove to avoid this. Fine, so long as you don't allow the fruit to become a mush.

HONEY SPONGE WITH A CHEESECAKE

Using honey is often a way to transform the familiar, just as substituting raw brown sugar for caster leaves people wondering what they are eating. This sponge is an excellent filler or accompaniment to a fruit dessert although some thought needs to be given to the flavour of the fruit to avoid it being overpowered by the sponge. We have done it with poached pears, but they were sometimes too bland. Raspberries or, better, loganberries and clotted cream are very desirable.

4 eggs	3oz / 75g caster sugar
4oz / 110g plain flour	3oz / 75g honey

Beat the eggs, sugar and honey together over a bowl of hot water until thick. Continue to beat for another 6 minutes. Fold in the flour and bake in a prepared sponge tin for about thirty minutes (180°C / 350°F / gas mark 4). When the sponge has cooled, split it and sprinkle each half with a syrup made with 2oz / 50g of honey and 5fl oz / 150ml of the juice or syrup of the fruit that you are to serve with it. Sandwich the sponge and top it with whipped cream.

An alternative use is as a sandwich for a cheesecake. This seems to convince the customer that cheesecake is worth trying again after years of manufactured confections. Make the sponge as detailed above and split it into three layers. Have ready also a syrup of honey and water as mentioned above. Make the cheesecake filling in the following manner:

6oz / 160g low fat cream cheese	1 egg white
2oz / 50g vanilla sugar	5fl oz / 150ml double cream
1 sheet gelatine	Grated rind of half a lemon
2 tablespoons lemon juice	

Dissolve the soaked gelatine in the lemon juice. Sieve the cream cheese and add the sugar and the grated rind. Mix in the lemon juice and gelatine. Whip the double cream lightly and the egg white stiffly. Have everything quite cold. Fold in the cream, then the egg white.

Take the bottom layer of the sponge and sprinkle it with syrup. Spread upon it half the cheesecake mixture. Press the next layer of sponge lightly upon it, sprinkle again, then the rest of the cheesecake, finishing with the third slice of sponge also sprinkled with the syrup. Wrap with clingfilm and leave for a few hours in the refrigerator. The sponge will take some of the moisture from the filling and the cake will firm up for slicing.

Hot desserts

STRAWBERRY PANCAKES

The pancake batter that has proved most satisfactory is that used in the
Savoy Hotel in London. It is higher in eggs and butter than most English
batters. One advantage of these proportions is that you can store the
pancakes without deterioration while many less rich require immediate
consumption. Equally, the high fat content makes them less prone to
sticking as well as easier to make thin.

17fl oz / 500ml milk   4oz / 110g unsalted butter
4 eggs   7oz / 200g flour

Beat the flour, eggs and half the milk together. Melt the butter and add it
to the mixture. Add the remainder of the milk, aiming for a thin cream
consistency. Too much beating, e.g. in a blender or electric machine,
does not improve the cooked texture. Leave to stand, beat before using.
Your pans should be hot, but not smoking. Cast iron, well seasoned,
works as well as non-stick, provided you sacrifice the first pancake. Pile
these up as they are made; ready for the filling and reheating that will
come when making the final dish. The quantities will do about sixteen
6in / 15cm pancakes.

A very good selection of batters is offered by Elisabeth Ayrton in *The
Cookery of England* (1975) including one very close to this. Many
recipes have cream and milk rather than milk alone; this adds even
greater luxury. Paul Bocuse, in *The New Cuisine* (1985) has another
good batter, for use with Grand Marnier. It has approximately double
the amount of butter and substitutes some of the milk with the liqueur.
This gives off a lovely smell as it is cooked. He also adds sugar. This may
be preferred by many when cooking a sweet thing, but it does tend to
toughen the pancake. Michel Guérard's *Cuisine Gourmande* (1978)
details 'Lazy Pancakes' which have a greater proportion of egg yolks to
whites but are otherwise very similar to the recipe above. He also adds
the grated zest of orange – another good idea if you are making
pancakes with an orange liqueur or oranges themselves.

Having made the pancakes, a mock cream is needed to go with the
strawberries in the filling.

Crème pâtissière

2 yolks of egg	2oz / 50g vanilla sugar
¾oz / 20g flour	10fl oz / 300ml milk

Mix the yolks, sugar and flour together with half the milk. Boil the rest of the milk and pour on to this mixture, stirring well. Return to the saucepan to cook very gently until the flour has cooked out. A *bain-marie* or double boiler will avoid overheating and spoiling the yolks.

To assemble the pancakes, lay them on a board and put a blob of the *crème pâtissière* on one quarter. Slice on to it some strawberries and fold the pancake into a triangle. Three pancakes per person should be sufficient. Put them on to a warmed and buttered flat dish, cover them with foil and leave them to warm in an oven (180°C / 350°F / gas mark 4) for about seven minutes. Before serving, dust them with icing sugar and flame them with Grand Marnier. You can, at this stage, show them a grill and brown the icing sugar. It is wise not to overfill the pancakes to avoid the contents leaking out.

BLACKBERRY PANCAKES WITH A SOUFFLÉ FILLING

Make a dozen pancakes according to the recipe given for strawberry pancakes (page 195). Select some very sweet cultivated blackberries which you can use raw, or wild blackberries that are ripe, have good flavour (not rain-sodden) and that have been cooked in a good syrup. Make a plain soufflé base.

¾oz / 20g butter	2½fl oz / 75ml *crème de myrtille*
½oz / 15g flour	(bilberry cordial), or *crème de*
2½fl oz / 75ml milk	*mûre* (blackberry cordial), or
1½oz / 45g vanilla sugar	the syrup from the
2 eggs	blackberries

Make a sauce by melting the butter, adding the flour and then the milk and the sugar. Cook the sauce out. Take off the heat. Separate the eggs, add the yolks to the cooling sauce, together with the cordial or syrup and beat to amalgamate. Whip the egg whites to a stiff peak. Fold into the soufflé base.

Lay out your pancakes and put a spoonful of soufflé mixture on to a half of each. Top this with three or four sweet blackberries. If you have had to cook some, ensure that they are well drained. Fold the pancakes in half. Put these on to a buttered cooking dish. Cover it with foil and bake in a hot oven (220°C / 425°F, gas mark 7) for five minutes. Dust with icing sugar, which may be glazed under a grill. Three pancakes are more than ample for a single serving.

PANCAKES WITH POMEGRANATE SAUCE AND PERSIMMON RUM CREAM

Pomegranates and persimmons are fruits that are easier to look at than to use. So often they are not ripe and will not ripen, although the variant of the persimmon, Sharon fruit, is sweeter. This simple recipe ensures that adjustment for sweetness can be made. There are no quantities necessary, it depends on your taste.

Use the pancake recipe given for strawberry pancakes. Make a pomegranate sauce to moisten these. Empty the pulp of a pomegranate into a sieve and press it through. Add a little white sugar and lemon juice and some grenadine, made itself from pomegranates. Reduce the mixture on the stove until syrupy.

The persimmon rum cream is made by extracting the flesh of a fruit, adding lemon juice, a little dark rum and brown sugar and liquidising these together. Then add some whipped double cream. Too much rum and the taste of the persimmon vanishes.

CHRISTMAS PUDDING — 'ELIZA ACTON'S'

We might be considered experts on Christmas puddings. Certainly, enough have been made to feed a thousand banquets. We have even exported them to France. This does not mean that our recipe is better than anyone else's. Its advantages, however, are that it is light and the taste of the ingredients does seem to come through. Too many puddings end up dark oak in colour and in taste. The base on which we worked is Eliza Acton's in *Modern Cookery* (1849 edn).

Puddings like this keep very well, so long as they are cooked sufficiently, that their resting place is cool and dry, and that they are well sealed. However, I do not think there is much virtue in long keeping. Christmas puddings do not taste any better for it. If they receive further boilings during the months of storage, to ensure sterility, then they will be merely darker and less distinctive. This may be to the taste of many people, but it is not in itself better. Mould growth is one of the bugbears of pudding making. Normally this is not harmful, but one is never entirely confident of one's devil-may-care attitude. If the pudding is left uncovered after it has been cooked the first time, this gives an opportunity for spores to settle on the surface. So we are especially scrupulous about the cooling, cleaning and sealing process. We have also found that aluminium foil bowls, even when coated, are not perfect containers for the long keeping of puddings made to this recipe. The acids in the fruit and citrus content eat through the foil. The safest bowl is a plastic one with a hermetically sealed lid. There is then no need to uncover the pudding at all once it has been placed in the boiler. China basins look more traditional, but are more difficult to cover.

For a 3lb / 1.3kg pudding:

3oz / 75g flour	2oz / 50g preserved stem ginger
3oz / 75g soft white breadcrumbs	2fl oz / 60ml brandy
	3 eggs
6oz / 150g shredded suet	4oz / 110g apples, peeled and cored weight
8oz / 225g raisins or sultanas	
8oz / 225g currants	Rind and juice of half an orange and half a lemon
6oz / 150g white sugar	
Half a teaspoon respectively of nutmeg and mace, ground	Good pinch of salt

Grate the rind and squeeze the juice of the citrus fruit. Peel and core the apples, weigh and chop. Chop the ginger. Beat the eggs.

Weigh out the dry ingredients and combine in a bowl. Mix thoroughly with hands, first without adding any liquids, then with them.

Wash a pudding basin and lightly oil it. Put in the mixture and cover it. Place it in a steamer or double boiler and cook for at least six hours, until the colour has turned. Ensure that you never run out of water.

The pudding will require at least two hours' boiling when you come to reheat it for consumption.

Stores and constants

BRIOCHE AND ENRICHED DOUGHS

A bread or bun enriched with eggs, butter and milk can be a useful base for a number of recipes. It can also be a change for tea and makes good rich toast if cosseting is needed. Such doughs make better sippets too; a practice now largely forgotten, but worth reviving. A round of toasted brioche makes a good base for a first course such as scallops with a saffron cream, or underneath some bone marrow, sent as an accompaniment to a steak. Using a brioche quite transforms a commonplace dish like bread and butter pudding. Such doughs also keep, especially if to be toasted before eating.

The brioche dough which has been found most satisfactory follows the instructions by Elizabeth David in *English Bread and Yeast Cookery* (1977).

6oz / 160g butter
3 eggs
¼oz / 7g yeast
2 tablespoons milk

10oz / 275g strong flour
1 teaspoon salt
1 tablespoon sugar

Soften the butter; beat the eggs lightly; cream the yeast and milk. Mix the flour, salt and sugar together; add the liquids and mix to a soft dough. Allow to rise in a warm spot, covered, for 90 minutes. Knock down and leave to rise overnight in a cool place, such as a larder.

It is not beyond most of our abilities to produce a reasonable brioche, but it does consume a lot of time. There is a recipe for 'French bread' by Elizabeth Moxon in *English Housewifery Exemplified* (1741) which results in an enriched loaf that may be an admirable first reserve for it takes no time at all. I have used the edited and modernised instructions given by Peter Brears in his *Gentlewoman's Kitchen* (1985), an excellent discussion of Yorkshire cooking in the seventeenth and eighteenth centuries.

1½lb / 675g strong flour
Good pinch of salt
3 yolks and 2 whites of egg

½oz / 15g yeast
1 pint / 600ml warm milk

Cream the yeast in the milk and beat in the eggs. Mix slowly into the flour. It is a *very* slack mixture so it is easier to use a spoon.

Butter or oil three 1pt / 600ml basins and divide the dough betwen them. An alternative is to use wooden bowls (the original method) that have been well floured. Leave to rise in the basins for between fifteen and thirty minutes. You should have a very warm spot for this rise, and it is sensible to have the ingredients and the bowls warm as well.

Turn out the dough onto a hot greased baking sheet and bake for 15 minutes at 230°C / 450°F / gas mark 8, then turn them for another ten minutes at 200°C / 400°F / gas mark 6.

FUDGE

A commodity that often seems easier on paper than in the flesh. This one works, but not invariably. There are many wrong turnings that can be taken but, in general, it works. For a large tray, suitable for a bring-and-buy:

2lbs / 900g granulated sugar	5fl oz / 150ml cold water
1 large tin evaporated, unsweetened, milk	8oz / 225g butter

Dissolve the ingredients in a large saucepan and take them to 'soft ball' on the sugar thermometer. Take off the heat, allow to cool somewhat and beat until there are signs of crystallisation. When these signs are advanced, hastened as they are by beating, pour the fudge into a well-greased tray. Let it set to such a point as will allow a knife to cut it cleanly into squares. Left too long, it will fracture rather than cut. Too early, the knife will clog as it passes through. Break or cut into pieces when it has cooled completely.

Comments on method could be extensive. Each week a variant to the normal behaviour of the mixture seems to show itself. More hot air has been exhausted on the subject of fudge than almost anything else. Among the more pertinent observations are these. A solid-top cooker makes better fudge than an open flame or ring that promote burnt pans. A wide saucepan, too, allows the water to evaporate quickly and the fudge to come up to temperature as quickly as possible. The pan should have a thick bottom and no hot spots. It is necessary, yet sometimes difficult, to ensure that the sugar has dissolved before you expose the mixture to too much heat, otherwise, the result will be granular. It is also necessary to take the fudge to true 'soft ball'. For a long time, it seems to teeter on the brink of 'soft ball' and the temptation is to take it off too early. Disaster is the result of such action.

Stir the fudge all the time it is cooking. This will lengthen the time it takes to attain its temperature, but keep it from sticking or burning. Burnt fudge is not unpleasant to eat, indeed it tastes more interesting that way; a burnt saucepan is not even very difficult to clean; but you will probably prefer not to burn it. One drawback of burning the mixture is evident when you come to cut it up. The small nodules of caramelised fudge stick to the knife as you draw it through – wreaking havoc on the still soft confection. Many instructions advise you to beat the fudge for five minutes after you have taken it from the heat. This is to give a creamy texture and to hasten crystallisation. If it is not beaten, it will crystallise on the top but not underneath and the end result will be grainy. However, I am not convinced that constant wearisome stirring has that dramatic an effect. Regular attention, stirring in bursts, seems often to be as beneficial. The tray in which the fudge is spread must be well greased. There is nothing more frustrating than a good batch being incapable of extraction. Some do not put it into a tray, rather they use a marble slab, containing the spread with heavy confectioners' bars.

There are many variations to the basic recipe. Indeed, it is almost too sweet and neutral as it stands. The most obvious is to use vanilla sugar. Or, as the fudge cools but before it is turned out, you can add a liqueur: Tia Maria, Grand Marnier or Drambuie. The former is the best. Different sorts of sugar can be used. A really black raw sugar makes a bitter fudge with a crumbly and soft texture. It is quite difficult to make this satisfactorily without the addition of some white sugar (about 25 per cent). A light brown muscovado is also good. The advantage of raw sugars is that they avoid that piercing sweetness that comes from granulated or caster.

CHOCOLATE CARAMELS

We once employed as Joyce Molyneux's assistant Nigel Marriage, coming to us after a long stint in the Savoy Hotel where he had worked in that part of the kitchen devoted to sweets and desserts. His tales of scale and grandeur would dumbfound us, cooking for twenty or thirty souls. Withal, he was well trained and good. He taught us to make these soft caramels, a good alternative to fudge.

7oz / 200g granulated sugar	5fl oz / 150ml water
7oz / 200g liquid glucose	5fl oz / 150ml double cream
(obtainable from a	5oz / 140g plain chocolate
pharmacist)	

Mix together the glucose, sugar and water, stirring to ensure dissolution as it heats. Add the double cream and boil to 'soft ball' on a sugar thermometer. Add the chocolate broken into small pieces. Stir repeatedly as it cools. Pour onto a well-oiled tray. Cut into squares when it has cooled completely.

SPICED LEMON PICKLE

This is an admirable pickle or chutney, a combination of sharp and sweet with palpable fruit content. It goes well with anything, particularly chicken croquettes and curries.

2lb / 900g lemons	2oz / 50g green ginger
1lb / 450g onions	2 large fresh green chillies
1 pint / 600ml wine vinegar	1 tablespoon whole allspice
1½lb / 675g granulated sugar	1 dessertspoon whole cardamom
1oz / 25g salt	1 dessertspoon whole coriander

Bag up the three spices in a muslin. Peel and grate the ginger. Deseed the chillies and chop finely. Squeeze the lemons and slice them thinly. Peel the onions and slice them as well. Mix the onion and lemon slices in a large bowl with the lemon juice, the vinegar, the chillies, green ginger and spices. Allow to steep overnight.

The next day, cook everything gently for about one and a half hours until the lemon skins are really tender. Once the sugar is added they will soften no more. Add the sugar, stir until dissolved and boil briskly for twenty minutes. Use a wide and solid saucepan. Pot up in jars with vinegar-proof lids and leave for at least a month before eating. It will keep almost indefinitely.

FRUIT CAKE

Restaurants do not cook fruit cakes. If they do, it is for their own consumption. The exception at Dartmouth was a recipe for Christmas, based on the rich fruit cake in Margaret Costa's *Four Seasons' Cookery Book* (1970). A few were made for customers and many for export to France. However, the mixture that is eaten most often at home is from instructions brought back by my wife from Australia. One might tell this from the inclusion of the tin of crushed pineapple. The end result is a very moist, sweet cake that disappears as fast as it is produced.

1 cup sugar

13oz / 375g tin of crushed
  pineapple

8oz / 225g raisins

8oz / 225g sultanas

1 teaspoon bicarbonate of soda

1 teaspoon mixed ground spices

4oz / 110g butter

1 cup plain flour

1 cup self raising flour

2 eggs

Put into a saucepan the sugar, pineapple, dried fruits, bicarbonate, spices and butter. Bring to the boil and boil for three minutes. Cool completely. Sift the flours together and fold into the mixture with two eggs, well beaten. Put in a lined and greased eight-inch tin. Bake at 170°C / 323°F / gas mark 3 for ninety minutes. Reduce the heat and leave for another twenty minutes until the knife comes out clean.

INDEX